EDITED

THE

RUSSELL
BOULTER

LIFELINES

EDITED BY CHRIS GIDNEY

THE STORY OF
RUSSELL
BOULTER

Marshall Pickering

An Imprint of HarperCollinsPublishers

Marshall Pickering is an Imprint of HarperCollins*Religious*
part of HarperCollins*Publishers*
77–85 Fulham Palace Road, London w6 8jb
www.christian-publishing.com

First published in Great Britain in 1999
by HarperCollins*Publishers*

10 9 8 7 6 5 4 3 2 1

A catalogue record for this book
is available from the British Library

ISBN 0 551 03211 1
Printed and bound in Great Britain by
Caledonian International Book Manufacturing Ltd, Glasgow

"Mark's Gospel is a direct and tough account of the life of Jesus." So says Russell Boulter, the actor who plays the part of Detective Sergeant John Boulton, a hard-nosed cop in the TV police series *The Bill.* "It's the shortest of the four Gospels, and it's possible to read it in an afternoon, like a mini-novel. I know – I've done it! It pulls no punches, and it's an ideal place to start if you've never read the Bible before, and you want to get straight down to the heart of the matter. I like it."

The Bill has become British television's most popular cop series. It is famed for its realistic "fly-on-the-wall" style of filming, and its strong characters add pace to what would otherwise be a very mundane police station. DS Boulton is one of the newest individuals to emerge. An aggressive but fair-minded detective, he enjoys cornering villains and being the hero, but he sometimes gets himself into some pretty difficult situations in the process. Spending much of his time driving police cars at breakneck speed up and down Balham High Street in London, where the series is filmed, Russell has nearly crashed on more than one occasion.

Originally auditioning for a part in 1992, Russell eventually appeared in one episode. The producers liked him and immediately offered him a permanent role. However, he had just signed a contract to appear in a Carla Lane series called *Luv* for the BBC, and so he was unable to accept the offer. A year later he was offered another part in the series, and once again he had to turn it down because he wanted to play a part in a production of Shakespeare's *Hamlet*. He promised himself that if a part in *The Bill* was offered to him a third time he would not turn it down, and so when the phone rang again, DS Boulton was finally written into the programme.

All the characters on *The Bill* are carefully balanced, but as Russell observes, "They wanted a cop who was a bit nastier, so they chose me!" In fact the concept behind DS Boulton in that first episode was that the officer had witnessed a colleague being shot dead, with the result that he became traumatized by the event and emerged as a vigilante. Russell explains, "He was ruthless because it was a way of overcoming his grief." This was an acceptable motive for Boulton for the first episode, but in order to avoid falling into the trap of becoming a pantomime "baddie", Russell had to invent stronger reasoning behind his character to keep him "alive" and "real". He decided that Boulton is the sort of policeman who is completely obsessed with justice, to the exclusion of everything else. In a very dangerous world for a policeman to be in, he sees things in very "black-and-white" terms, with little room for mercy. Occasionally, though, just to make him a bit different and to keep the character interesting, Russell enjoys the opportunity to get Boulton to do something nice.

Of course, it's often down to the screen-writers to decide which way the character is going to behave in any given situation, and it's Russell's job to interpret this. It's a bit like putting the flesh and clothing onto a skeleton. If the crime is a complex one, Boulton tends to display a lot of frustration and slips into his rude and callous old nature. It seems that the female writers tend to hate his character and bring out his aggression more, but the male writers prefer to show him in a better light. Russell jokingly says, "If I see a woman's name on the front of the script when it arrives, I know that I'm going to get hit. If a man has written the script, I know that my character will hit someone else!"

The mailbag at the production offices is full every day. Often the letters are from viewers who say how much they like DS Boulton. Strangely, the majority of these letters are from women. This is a surprise to Russell. Sometimes the ladies who write to him make some very strange requests – some have even asked him to come to their homes and arrest them!

The appeal of the series, which has run for more than 10 years now, is probably due to the fact that most of the crimes have to be solved within half an hour. This means that there is a lot of action, which is one reason why Russell likes being in the show. Even with the introduction of the new one-hour "specials", they have managed to keep the action going. He has always enjoyed playing characters who do things rather than just talk. In an age when men are often struggling to find their role in society, Russell finds it quite refreshing to play this type of individual, who is able to do things that most men would never be allowed to get away with!

Home life is a comfortable place of escape for Russell, who is now recognized wherever he goes. Earlier in his acting career he used to be able to walk down the street and go shopping without being noticed. Now he wears a hat if he doesn't want to be disturbed. When Russell goes out, there is little privacy to be had.

Russell commutes each day to wherever *The Bill* happens to be filming. It may seem like a glamorous lifestyle, but the reality is that it can be extremely exhausting keeping up with the filming schedules of a series like *The Bill*. Russell will often arrive on set at 4 a.m. or earlier, will be transported to several different locations throughout the day, and will finish with a night shoot, arriving home late, only to get up early the next day.

There is a lot of pressure to learn lines very quickly, and when he is not on camera Russell will be found hiding in a corner somewhere, going through the rest of the day's script. When you are contracted to a television company, there are times when it seems that you are at the mercy of the programme's director. Russell can be called to work any day or night, and this plays havoc with his personal and social life, not to mention his church life!

A Bible under the bed

Russell became a Christian in 1981 at All Souls Church, Langham Place, London, during an invitation service. The preacher was Eric Delve and the title of the sermon was "Everything you have always wanted to know about God, but were afraid to ask".

Russell, aged 18, was in his first term of a three-year drama course at the London Academy of Musical and Dramatic Art (LAMDA). He was following his dream of becoming an actor. He never felt more "alive" than when standing on stage in front of an audience.

His first impressions of drama school had been disappointing. Any egotistical feelings he might have had were quickly squeezed out by all the hard work that was involved in the disciplined training of an actor. There had been 800 applicants for 30 places, and those who had got the places were under pressure to prove themselves. Russell enjoyed the course, but he didn't know anyone in London, so in his first term he found himself spending a lot of time alone. This left him feeling confused, and he even felt unsure that he had chosen the right career.

At about the same time, Russell was given a Bible by his uncle, who had recently become a Christian. Aware that his uncle would be fervently praying for him, Russell obediently read this Bible at bedtime each night at the hostel where he was staying, but to avoid being seen as "religious" by the other people there, he used to read it by torchlight under his bedsheets!

He was worried about being seen as interested in God partly because all the Christians he had met up to this point had been "dorks"! He had found it very hard to relate to them. And yet the Jesus whom he was reading about each night struck him as an amazing character, and he wondered why nobody had told him about Jesus before.

"I read the Gospels as I would have read a novel," says Russell, "and, frankly, I was shocked! The Jesus I had been told about at school wore a nightie and floated a few feet off the ground, but the Jesus I was now reading about was interesting and relevant to my own life. He was dangerous and exciting. He turned over the money-changers' tables, he called religious hypocrites 'sons of snakes', and he healed broken-hearted people. He was accused of being a drunkard at wedding parties, of hanging out with prostitutes and lepers. He cast out devils, he had authority, he was brave, fearsome and passionate, and I really liked him!

"This caused me a problem, because I considered myself to be an atheist, and the Jesus I liked quite clearly described himself as the Son of God." Russell decided that if all that was claimed about this Jesus was false, it was the biggest lie in history. But if it was true, it was worth finding out more about Jesus.

He then noticed the verse, "Ask, and you will receive" (Matthew 7:7). Thinking it only fair to take this Jesus at his word, Russell prayed and asked the question, "If you are God and you love us, why do you allow so much suffering and evil? If you are good you would stop it. So do you exist?"

"I didn't expect a reply," recalls Russell, "but the next day I received a book in the post from my uncle. It was by C. S. Lewis and was entitled *God in the Dock*. It made me smile to think that I had received such a quick answer."

In it Russell read Lewis' argument that God *does* oppose evil but will not violate our freedom. We are free to love or to hate. He will not turn us into machines. If we lived as God suggested, then there would be a massive decrease in suffering, as most suffering is caused by human beings. If you don't believe in God, and therefore believe that there is no absolute right or wrong and that the universe is without meaning, then why is suffering and evil a problem for you anyway? Russell had to admit that it was a pretty good answer.

The next morning, walking from his digs through central London to drama school, he asked God his next question: "How do I know that you are really there, and not just in my imagination? Why won't you *say* something to me?"

Russell remembers that "As I walked along I felt a suggestion slip into my thoughts: 'Look to your left.' I did, and I saw a poster on a church notice-board. It said, 'If you don't understand my silence, how will you understand when I speak?' Touché!"

From then on Russell started to actively seek out God, although, looking back, he now thinks that God was actually looking for him. He still had a lot of questions, mostly to do with his fears about what God was really like. Russell's brain constantly juggled with thoughts such as "Does God really care about me? Does he want to annihilate my personality? Is he just playing games with the universe? If I become a Christian, will my friends reject me?" He needed to find answers to these questions before he could really believe.

One rainy day

Being new to London, Russell was unsure of his way around the big city but was unwilling to carry an A-to-Z map in case people thought he was a tourist. Consequently he often had problems finding his way among the streets and bars and shops, and one day he got completely lost. As he struggled to work out which direction was the best way to go, it suddenly started to rain. He had no money on him, and so he felt a little low in spirit. Then he noticed a huge church up ahead. He remembers that as he walked past the church, a strange sensation came over him. "It really felt like God was telling me to go into the church and pray," he says, "but I pushed the idea away as being utterly ridiculous, and kept on walking." Soon after that the rain started to fall heavily, and before long Russell was soaked to the skin. He didn't know which way to turn, and, standing there in the cold rain, he heard himself praying a simple prayer for help. Again it seemed that a clear voice in his head was speaking, this time telling him to turn to the right. He duly turned right and walked down a street, and was amazed to see in front of him the same huge church that he had passed more than an hour ago.

Entering the empty building, he sat down and flicked through a leaflet that had been left on the seat after a recent service. The interior was bright and modern with an impressive pulpit of moulded steel, and Russell felt strangely at home there. The leaflet was an invitation to a forthcoming "guest service", and Russell decided that he should make an effort to attend. Despite his recent experiences, he was still not convinced about the reality of God, but he continued to talk to him in a very forthright manner. He continually threw questions heavenwards on subjects such as evolution, creation and even the Spanish Inquisition! He promised that if God helped him to understand these questions, he would then start to take God seriously.

He kept the invitation to the guest service in his pocket, and it reminded him that he had decided to attend. On the Sunday morning, expecting the church to be embarrassingly quiet through lack of interest, he was astounded when, as he turned the corner, he saw a huge throng of people queuing to get inside. Thinking that he might not get a seat, he quickly joined the queue and went in.

Eventually he found himself sitting amongst a thousand people. A sense of eager expectation filled the air. After a series of rousing hymns, accompanied by one of the best orchestras Russell had ever heard, everyone settled down to listen to the sermon. Russell had always assumed that this was traditionally the time when most people took the opportunity for an extra day-time nap.

As the preacher spoke, Russell was transfixed. This man, whom he had never met, seemed to be answering the questions that Russell had been fervently keeping to himself over the past few months.

The preacher then went on to talk about Christ's crucifixion. Russell had not yet got as far as this in his secret bedtime Bible reading. In the Gospels Russell found that there were three basic reactions to Jesus – terror or adoration or hatred. "No one in the Gospels mildly approved of Jesus," Russell explains. "He was not the 'meek and mild' character that people often think he was. He was actually a man of steel – someone you have no choice but to respond to."

As the reason behind the crucifixion was slowly unpacked by the man in the pulpit, it began to dawn on Russell that Jesus was not a wimp but was God himself reaching down to the human beings he had made. In Russell's mind the pieces of the spiritual jigsaw were slowly falling into place. It was a revelation to him when he realized that Jesus was not just a moral teacher but was the Son of God. Russell explains: "Jesus says, 'If you want to know what God is like, take a look at me. I'm what God is like.' Suddenly all my ideas of God as a boring, miserable person who just wanted to spoil everyone's fun were completely shattered. If God was like Jesus, that meant that I liked God, and I wanted to know him."

As the story continued to unfold it occurred to Russell that if Jesus was God he didn't have to put up with being treated in such a humiliating way. "He could have snapped his fingers at any time," says Russell, "and an army of angels would immediately have come to the rescue and blasted everyone! But then it hit me. He was doing it to pay for my sins towards God. I realized that I must matter a lot to God if Jesus was willing to go through all of that just so that I could know God, just so that the barrier between him and me could be broken. If he was prepared to pay that much of a ransom for me, then I really, really wanted to know him."

The preacher then asked all those who wanted to accept Jesus Christ into their lives to pray. But Russell was unaware that it was supposed to be a silent prayer, so he confidently shouted out his acceptance of Christ, which brought a smile to many faces. Russell says that something had changed – he felt almost physically different. As he puts it, "It was as if all that I believed about God on the outside was now somehow on the inside. I could feel God's love and acceptance within me. It made me feel incredibly confident and buoyant. I danced all the way home!"

When Monday morning came, Russell was surprised to find that his feelings hadn't changed. He still felt that God was so close that he could reach out and touch him.

At drama school Russell was eager to tell his friends about what he had experienced over the weekend. Their reaction was not encouraging, however. They labelled their fellow student as someone who had finally "flipped".

Russell learned quickly that becoming a Christian does not make your life easier. In many ways his life became harder. But he says, "I still can't understand those who think that you suddenly become boring when you believe in God. For me, life became much more exciting. I've certainly had more fun since becoming a Christian. It was as if someone had switched the 'colour' switch on. My life had a meaning and a purpose at last. Nothing was pointless, and I was satisfied that I would not just be pushing up the daisies in 50 years' time. Everything I did was now important to God, and my relationship with him would last forever. It's all a bigger picture now."

The working man's Gospel

Russell admits that reading his Bible is not easy. Constantly being pushed for time, and without the security and routine of regular working hours, it's often a case of all or nothing. He will snatch a verse or two one day, and digest whole chapters another day. He considers it vital to have a healthy and balanced spiritual diet.

Russell calls Mark's Gospel "the working man's Gospel", not because it has anything to do with class, but because it is the sort of biography that relates to the here and now. It may have been written nearly 2,000 years ago, but its message and its challenge are still relevant. Culture may have changed, but humanity has not. People today are still faced with the same age-old basic problems that people faced when Mark's Gospel was written.

"Do you want to know what God is like?" repeats Russell. "Then look at Jesus. As you read the Gospel of Mark, Jesus' humanity is startlingly clear. He gets tired, angry and frustrated. He stands apart and observes, he is witty and dangerous and uncompromising. He is ruthless with hypocrites, and compassionate with the weak and lonely. He's a real man's man, and is nothing like those old pictures that make him look pale, weak and wishey-washey.

"When you read Mark for the first time, you immediately notice how different Jesus is from the 'meek and mild' image that the Victorians gave him. You can't fail to come nearer to Jesus by reading this Gospel. His magnetism, his strength, his love just melt away any barriers inside, and you find yourself being inextricably drawn closer. As an actor, I find him the most fascinating figure in history. As a person I find him to be the best mate I have ever had. He never lets me down, and he always knows what is best for me. He's always there too, and never bunks off to the pub when I'm feeling in need of a bit of support. Most of all, he never rejects me for who or what I am."

For Jesus there was no such thing as class or taboo. In fact he seemed to enjoy treading on the toes of the religious leaders of the day, and he spent time with those who were normally alienated by society. This included women, lepers, tax collectors and Roman citizens. He also talked to an insane hermit, a young boy, a housewife, a criminal, a king, a blind beggar and many more.

What impresses Russell the most about Jesus in Mark's Gospel is the challenge that he gave his listeners when he told the Parable of the Sower in Chapter 4. Russell is a great lover of short stories, and he feels that Jesus made brilliant use of dramatic parables as a means of communicating his message. Russell thinks Jesus must have displayed amazing personal dynamism to keep his audiences hanging on his every word for hours on end. Russell wishes that a time machine could transport him back 2,000 years so that he could see the master storyteller at work!

In Jesus, Russell can see many of the marks of his own profession, such as voice projection and the ability to draw a crowd. Not that he's calling Jesus an actor, of course. That would belittle Jesus and would suggest that he was just an entertainer. No, for Russell Jesus is definitely someone unique with the most important and life-changing message that anyone will ever hear. Jesus challenges us to put his words into action and see for ourselves if they are true. Russell comments, "It's not true that Christianity has been tried and found wanting. Often it has never been tried in the first place."

In the Parable of the Sower Jesus talks about the seed falling on many different types of soil. Some seed falls on the path, some falls on rocky ground, some falls among thorn bushes, and some falls in good soil. The "seed" is really God's message, God's word, but it's not just for those who are hearing God's call for the first time. Russell has experienced the four soils for himself and admits that there are times when he responds differently to God's message, even though he has been a Christian for quite a while now. "I'm sure we all experience those times when we willingly accept God's word in some areas of our lives and resist it in others. You may be open to God about your career, but closed concerning how you spend your money. I might respond like good soil to the thought of praying, but like rocky soil when it comes to reading my Bible."

An old-fashioned word

Mark's Gospel is so full of parables and challenges that it would be easy to see Jesus as someone like a police sergeant barking out a series of rules and regulations for his officers to obey – maybe even taking a sadistic delight in seeing his men flounder as they try to perform tasks that are impossible to achieve. Not so with Jesus, says Russell. His rules are there for our own protection. The purpose of traffic lights is to prevent road accidents. In a similar way, God gave us rules to follow so that we can avoid personal disaster. If you go through a red traffic light, you are likely to pay a high price for your disobedience – a damaged car, injury or even death. Likewise, disobeying God has its own consequences. "It's not that God is there with a big stick, ready to hit us when we get it wrong," explains Russell. "It's just that when we decide to step out from under his protection and go it alone, we put ourselves in danger."

Disobeying God is referred to in the Bible by the old-fashioned word "sin". Originally this was a word used by archers and meant missing the target they were aiming at. Like the golfer who shouts "Fore!" when the ball goes speeding off in the wrong direction, the archer would shout "Sinner!" and everyone would take a dive. The Bible makes it clear that we are all "sinners" – we have all missed the mark. Even those who claim never to have done any wrong cannot claim, for example, that they have never had a jealous thought about their neighbour or friend. It's also no good hiding behind the excuse that because we are just human beings we are prone to failure. Committed Christians believe that with God's help, it is possible to live in a Christlike way.

For the person who has accepted God into their life, the cost of sin has already been met. "It's as if you've just gone through a red light and smashed into another car," explains Russell, "and then someone comes along and pays for the repairs and the fine as well! To use another old-fashioned word, 'salvation' is the antidote to sin. They may be very old words, but they are just as important today as they ever were. Salvation is a free gift, but it isn't cheap. Jesus died on the cross so that we could have it. To receive it you have to give everything you are to God."

Russell enjoys digging and delving into the scriptures to see how they relate to his everyday life. "Another of my favourite bits of Mark's Gospel is in Chapter 2, where Jesus is having dinner at the house of a friend, Levi the tax collector. The local religious leaders slag him off because he's eating with 'sinners', to which he replies, 'People who are well do not need a doctor, but only those who are sick. I have not come to call respectable people, but outcasts.'

"I think it's sad that so many people stay away from Jesus and Christianity because they feel that they aren't 'good enough', that they are too sinful. There are many people who have no trouble in believing in God, but they just think that God is unforgiving, that they just aren't good enough to know him and that only 'perfect, religious' people can be Christians.

"The irony is that the feeling of not being good enough is the very thing that qualifies you to believe in Jesus in the first place! Who bothers to go to a doctor if they feel fine? Jesus is perfectly at ease sitting at a table eating with sinners, and he would be perfectly at ease with you. You have no need to impress him. You don't have to be perfect to be a Christian. Jesus is keen to get to know you, just as you are right now, with no huge effort on your part to become religious or perfect or even good."

Actors live in a strange, upside-down world. They go to work when most people come home, they go to bed when others are just getting up, and they work hardest when the rest of us are taking a holiday. After doing a show it's often impossible for a performer to go straight home and to bed – he or she needs to unwind first. The ideal way to do this is to enjoy a meal with friends – often until very late at night!

Russell smiles at the fact that Jesus was called a glutton and a drunkard by the Pharisees who hated him.

"I imagine Jesus was called these things because he was always eating and drinking with people. From the moment when he was born around the back of an inn to the final supper he had with his disciples, food and fellowship were obviously important to Jesus. He loved to share a meal and a chat, and would have been well at home in one of our after-show dinners. He enjoyed answering the many questions that people asked him, and he still encourages us to ask him our questions now. He wants us to seek him out, to knock on his door. So, as my uncle said to me when he first gave me that Bible, 'Don't let other people tell you what to think. Find out for yourself.'"

Not a Bible-basher

It's Russell's experience that many of his fellow actors are intrigued by his Christianity. He is not a Bible-basher and prefers to encourage them to "find out for themselves" rather than taking every opportunity to preach at them. While he has been working on *The Bill* his faith has been noticed. As he was walking down the corridor of Sun Hill Police Station one day, he was confronted by a large actor who asked him if he was a Christian. When Russell said yes, the actor gave a huge smile and said that he was one too. They began to meet and pray for each other, often between "takes", leaning against a prop police car and sipping a cup of coffee.

On another occasion Russell found himself playing opposite an actor friend whom he knew to be a Christian. Lloyd had been cast as a black youth who had a particular distaste for the police. According to the script DS Boulton was meant to be very aggressive towards this character, and Russell found this surprisingly hard to do. "I knew this actor was a brother in Christ, and yet my character was treating his character with contempt and hatred," Russell explains. "We had to really work hard on the scene together to make it look realistic between us, and to overcome the natural respect that we had for each other."

Real Christian faith can never be kept secret, and before long Russell's colleagues on *The Bill* wanted to know what made him "tick". "Faith is something that a lot of people are hungry for," says Russell. "We often feel embarrassed by our Christian beliefs, and yet in my experience, people really want to know what I have got. When they see the solidity of what I believe, they are often more jealous than jeering."

Fellowship with other believers is important to Russell, but because of his working routine as an actor he finds that it is impossible to achieve on a regular basis. Since he is sometimes away from home on tour or location and often works unpredictable hours, it is very difficult for him to know when he will be able to get to church. This is why it is particularly rewarding when he finds himself working alongside another Christian in the business.

Some years ago, Russell was playing the lead in the highly successful West End musical *Blood Brothers*. An organization called Christians in Entertainment was holding a weekly Bible study nearby at Her Majesty's Theatre during the run of *The Phantom of the Opera*. Russell was unable to join them, as his matinée performance clashed with the time of the group's meeting. Russell decided to have a Bible study of his own, and CIE offered to support him. Each Thursday afternoon Russell and a pastor from CIE met backstage to read from the Bible together and to pray for each other and the show. The other performers couldn't understand why there was so much laughter emanating from Russell's dressing room! Their preconceptions about Christians being boring were slowly broken down. Other cast members joined them sometimes, particularly when they were facing difficulties and wanted prayer. Russell enjoyed the chance to be open about his faith.

It wasn't long before another meeting started up in the dressing room across the corridor from Russell's. A Buddhist believer on the show obviously thought that meeting with like-minded people was a good idea and had decided to follow suit. Every Saturday afternoon between the matinée and the evening performance chanting and incense issued from the room and flowed down the corridor. Russell was amused by this and did not feel at all threatened by the "opposition". In fact he was glad that his Bible study had shown that a spiritual dimension to life in the theatre was important and relevant.

The supposed glitz and glamour of show business hide the reality of loneliness and fear that lurks behind every script. Actors tend to be constantly worried about auditions, the suitability of their voice, face, hair or height, their acting ability and whether the director will like them or loathe them. Even when you have "made it", the concerns of the industry never subside. As a celebrity you have a greater responsibility to make sure that you never disappoint your public or your fellow performers, who will all be looking up to you. As in Chapter 4 of Mark's Gospel, where the disciples are in a boat on Lake Galilee, storms can suddenly and ferociously arise. The politics of a contract, a disagreement with your agent, the jealousy of your co-star or the fear of unemployment can arouse deep fears and send you into the depths of despair.

The disciples were afraid that they would drown in the storm, and they woke up the sleeping Jesus to save them. It has always amazed Russell that Jesus was actually asleep during the storm in the first place. He must have been so at peace with himself and his mission that even a storm could not disturb him. Obviously, the master wanted his disciples to have this same peace and to be confident with him, so he chided them, saying that their faith was very small.

Nevertheless, this incident reminds Russell that Jesus was, and is, the one with authority. Just as the astonished disciples saw the storm subside at Jesus' command, so Russell knows that many of the storms of fear that rise up within him can be calmed by the presence of God in his life. In practice this means praying in the wings before a show or on the way to a location. It's vital to Russell that God "owns" the day ahead before he tries to manage it by himself.

A man of action

Mark was the first of the four Gospels to be written, so the writer seems to concentrate on action rather than words. It's interesting to note that the other three Gospels quote all of Mark except for a mere 31 verses. Mark also records more miracles than any other Gospel. Jesus was obviously a man of action. He was usually on the move, and yet he was never too busy to stop for those who needed his help, like blind Bartimaeus in Chapter 10.

Russell reckons that Jesus must have travelled hundreds of miles in the last three years of his life. He went from town to town with his disciples, which reminds Russell of the many theatrical tours he has experienced in which the journeys were so exhausting. Jesus knew just what he was doing, however, and this perfect combination of moving and stopping speaks to Russell about his own life, which is constantly on the move. "I want God to move in my life," he says. "I don't want to be stagnant in my faith, my career or my emotions. All actors are passionate people and get bored very easily, and I want God to lead me on into new experiences that help me to grow."

And yet the times when Jesus stopped to rest can be a frustration to Russell, as relaxation is not always on the agenda for a busy actor. Even when an actor is unemployed, plans to get the next job are in full progress. For Russell, decorating his home is one way of winding down, but there is always the risk of ending up with a half-finished room with two different types of wallpaper!

In Chapter 1 of Mark's Gospel we read that Jesus went out in the early morning to pray so that he would not be bothered by the huge crowds that followed him. He needed to have some time when he could be alone with God, and he had become so famous that he had to take positive steps to protect his privacy. This was something that he would continue to practise throughout his life, right up to his solo, night-time prayers of anguish in the Garden of Gethsemane.

Work is almost a form of worship to the actor who enjoys his job. It's not just a job, of course, but a driving passion. Russell wants to push himself as much as possible and reach his highest potential, using the tools that God has given him. But he is aware that sometimes he is just too busy. "It's so easy to get into the treadmill of life, and it's so difficult to get off it," Russell comments. "What I have found is that God is loving, protective and easy to be with. I have a relationship in which God treats me with respect, even when I blow it. He is my teacher, guide and friend, and he is prepared to move heaven and earth to have a conversation with me when I am too busy to listen! This is more than I deserve."

On a recent visit to the Holy Land, where he had been making a film, Russell stayed on there for a while after the filming had been completed so that he could spend some time "being still" with God. In the midst of the place where Jesus himself had walked, he enjoyed some undisturbed time which, Russell says, was highly therapeutic for body, mind and soul.

Russell's visit to the Holy Land also had the effect of bringing the Bible to life for him. From Bethlehem to the Garden Tomb, the whole experience was mind-blowing.

Russell was especially struck by the fact that when Jesus made his triumphal entry into Jerusalem, he rode not in a splendid chariot or on a mighty war-horse, but on a humble donkey. Despite being the Son of God, the creator of the world and the answer to all of humankind's problems, Jesus came in humility.

This is not a word that is often associated with show business! Russell finds that there is a difference between egotism and self-confidence, and a balance needs to be struck between them. "It's important as an actor to believe in yourself," he says. "You have to convince yourself that you are the best – otherwise you would never be capable of facing 200 other people at an audition, all applying for the same part! It's when pride comes in that the problems occur. When you stop admitting that you have been given a gift to use, and start thinking that you are the creator of the gift yourself, then you start to shut others out, including God."

On the lookout

Russell laughs when he thinks about how many people he bumps into on a daily basis. "I think I may become a professional socialite one day," he grins. "It's a small world – I always seem to be meeting people who I have worked with in the past. I believe that God leads me to

meet certain people, sometimes so that I can share something about my faith." He is a great believer in "divine appointments" and is always on the lookout to see what God's purpose for him each day will be. It often seems that he bumps unexpectedly into old friends when they are going through hard times, and this gives Russell the opportunity to bring them some comfort and encouragement.

Encouragement is a particularly important spiritual gift which is often underestimated, but it is always welcomed by others. Russell has this gift and is able to use it with much effect. He has been through his own hard times too. When there was no money left to buy even a loaf of bread, his sense of hope in God pulled him through. "Every actor lives by faith," he says. "You have to trust God that there will be a job waiting for you around the corner." Having experienced life on the breadline, he fondly remembers times when the money came in on just the right day to pay the bills. He says difficulties in his personal life and confusion over his career have all been helped by his relationship with God.

"'Trusting in God is essential," Russell says. When he is questioned about his faith, he is often asked how he can believe in a God he cannot see, hear or touch. "I can see him at work in my life and in the lives of others," he replies. "I can hear God speaking to me in so many ways

that it sometimes seems almost audible. I may not be able to reach out and physically touch God, but I have known God's touch upon my life without a doubt.

"Faith is important, because God does not want to force us into believing in Him. If, in the middle of filming *The Bill* one day, a huge foot came down from heaven, we would all be forced to believe in God. But that's not faith! If he made us acknowledge him, we would be no more than puppets without any freedom whatsoever.

"When people say to me that surely there are many ways of reaching God, I have to point back to the Bible, and especially to Mark's Gospel. Jesus said, and showed, quite simply that he was the only way to Father God. My house has one pathway leading up to my front door. I only need one. If I had several it would probably be very confusing for those who come to visit. 'Which path should I take?' they would say. 'Which way is the shortest? Which way is the right one?' No, I only need one pathway to my house, and everyone can rely on the fact that it leads right up to my front door, with no diversions. I know that the pathway to God lies in our relationship with Jesus Christ and his death on the cross."

The biggest buzz

Despite all the supposed glamour and excitement of being a celebrity working in the entertainment industry, Russell is eager to underline the fact that it is being a Christian that gives him the biggest "buzz" in his life. However, he still enjoys his work immensely. Eric Liddell, the British champion athlete whose story was told in the film *Chariots of Fire*, said, "I believe God made me for a purpose, but he also made me fast, and when I run I feel his pleasure." Russell is confident that the gifts that God has given him are there to be used, not wasted; that there is nothing wrong in enjoying where God has put us; that we should blossom where we have been planted.

"When I became a Christian the most exciting thing for me was being in church. The fantastic feeling I got from being in the presence of God was more powerful than standing in front of any audience." Just after becoming a Christian, Russell was convinced that God would want him to give up the business and become a missionary or a preacher, and he constantly prayed that God would show him what to do. "Every time I prayed for guidance I got cast in some fantastic part the next day! In the end I knew that what God wanted me to do was to be an actor."

When asked if he feels whether acting is an appropriate career for a Christian, Russell says, "I think the question for the previous generation of Christians who wanted to pursue an acting career was 'Dare I use this talent for God?' The question for my generation is 'Dare I *not* use this talent for God?'"

For Russell, being an actor without God in his life would be extremely boring. It's the mixture of faith and work that makes Russell's life exciting. Russell thinks that the surprising thing about God is that he's there when you don't expect it. "Maybe you think you've left him in church on Sunday, but then he turns up at work just when you're being crabby!" he laughs. "I learnt that God's fine so long as you're honest with him. There's no point in trying to somehow make yourself 'righteous' enough to talk to God. It's silly to think that God will accept me more today if I'm a nicer person. The fact is, we've all blown it, and we need to meet with God exactly where we are. Mark's Gospel helps me to do that."

Apparently even Christians "blow it". During a recent mission conducted by the Argentinian evangelist Luis Palau, it was surprising that more people came forward to recommit themselves to God than came to meet him for the first time. Many who, for one reason or another, find themselves drifting away from their relationship with

God soon realize that a successful life without God is impossible, and they wake up and see what is missing.

It's also obvious that more and more people are coming to understand the importance and reality of a spiritual dimension to life. There is a great spiritual hunger in our society, and people are searching for a meaning to their existence. Russell thinks they often look in the wrong direction. "If my watch is broken, I may take it to the butcher's, the baker's and the candlestick maker's, but none of them will be able to repair it. I have to take my watch back to the watchmaker, the one who created it in the first place. He knows the intricacies of the watch and what makes it tick. He is able to repair it and make it as good as new."

Russell agrees that we live at a time when it is not easy to be a Christian. He thinks the problem is not really that Christians get laughed at by their friends; the real difficulty is simply that Christians often have to swim against the tide of popular society. Governments realize the importance of morality in our culture and so struggle to provide moral guidelines, but they just get accused of trying to create a "nanny state". People seem to want to have the freedom to do whatever they wish without having to face the consequences. Russell believes that as a result, family, marriage and personal life are in a chaotic state. He says God's guidelines are there not to suffocate us but to protect us.

Russell's challenge to read Mark's Gospel is clear: "Put down your prejudices long enough to read this short Gospel, and you may be pleasantly surprised. At the very least, it's a great read. And who knows? You could get to meet the best friend you'll ever have."

So what's at the heart of Christianity for Russell? "God loves you. It's as simple as that. Mark's Gospel makes that abundantly clear. Forget religion. God, the creator of this universe, loves you. There is no one else like you; you are utterly unique. God's only got one you, and he loves you. End of story."

Russell's prayer

Riches I need not, nor man's empty praise.
You are my inheritance through all of my days.
You and You only, first in my heart,
High King of Heaven, my treasure You are.
Be my vision, O Lord, I pray.

(adapted from 'Be Thou my vision' from *The Poem Book of the Gael*, selected and edited by Eleanor Hull)

Russell's favourite moments in Mark's Gospel

- *Jesus the Tough Man*: Mark 8:11–13; 11:15–19; 14:53–65; 15:1–41.
- *Jesus the Compassionate Man*: Mark 10:13–16; 12:41–44.
- *Jesus the Communicator*: Mark 3:7–12; 4:1–34.
- *Jesus the Healer*: Mark 1:29–34, 40–45; 2:1–12; 3:1–6; 6:53–56; 7:31–37.
- *Jesus the Friend*: Mark 14:3–11.
- *Jesus the Strategist*: Mark 1:35–39; 14:32–42.
- *Jesus the Socialite*: Mark 2:13–17.

Further help

This book contains two stories. One is the story of Russell Boulter and the other is the story of Jesus Christ taken from Mark's Gospel in the Bible. There are millions of people around the world who, like Russell, say that discovering Jesus has changed their lives completely. If you would like to find out more, here are some suggestions:

- Talk to someone you know who is a practising Christian.

- Find a Bible and read some more (we have used the *Good News Bible* version of Mark's Gospel).
- Find a local church where people are willing to explain more about the Christian faith.
- Read some other books about people finding Jesus, such as *The Cross and the Switchblade* by David Wilkerson, *The Joni Story* by Joni Eareckson Tada and *Under the Influence* by Julia Fisher (all published by HarperCollins*Religious*).

Useful addresses

- Christian Enquiry Agency, Inter-church House, 35 Lower Marsh, London SE1 7RL. Tel: 0171 620 4444.
- Bible Society, Stonehill Green, Westlea, Swindon, Wilts. SN5 7DG. Tel: 01793 418100.
- Christians in Entertainment, PO Box 3019, South Croydon, Surrey CR2 7PJ.

THE STORY OF
JESUS
CHRIST

AS TOLD IN THE
GOSPEL OF MARK

Introduction

The Gospel according to Mark begins with the statement that it is "the Good News about Jesus Christ, the Son of God". Jesus is pictured as a man of action and authority. His authority is seen in his teaching, in his power over demons, and in forgiving people's sins. Jesus speaks of himself as the Son of Man, who came to give his life to set people free from sin.

Mark presents the story of Jesus in a straightforward, vigorous way, with emphasis on what Jesus did, rather than on his words and teachings. After a brief prologue about John the Baptist and the baptism and temptation of Jesus, the writer immediately takes up Jesus' ministry of healing and teaching. As time goes on, the followers of Jesus come to understand him better, but Jesus' opponents become more hostile. The closing chapters report the events of Jesus' last week of earthly life, especially his crucifixion and resurrection.

The two endings to the Gospel, which are enclosed in brackets, are generally regarded as written by someone other than the author of *Mark*.

Outline of Contents

The Preaching of John the Baptist

1 This is the Good News about Jesus Christ, the Son of God. [a] [2] It began as the prophet Isaiah had written: "God said, 'I will send my messenger ahead of you to clear the way for you.'

[3] Someone is shouting in the desert,

'Get the road ready for the Lord;

make a straight path for him to travel!'"

[4] So John appeared in the desert, baptizing and preaching.[b] "Turn away from your sins and be baptized," he told the people, "and God will forgive your sins."[5] Many people from the province of Judea and the city of Jerusalem went out to hear John. They confessed their sins, and he baptized them in the River Jordan.

a 1.1 *Some manuscripts do not have* the Son of God.
b 1.4 John appeared in the desert, baptizing and preaching; *some manuscripts have* John the Baptist appeared in the desert, preaching.

⁶ John wore clothes made of camel's hair, with a leather belt round his waist, and his food was locusts and wild honey. ⁷ He announced to the people, "The man who will come after me is much greater than I am. I am not good enough even to bend down and untie his sandals. ⁸ I baptize you with water, but he will baptize you with the Holy Spirit."

The Baptism and Temptation of Jesus

⁹ Not long afterwards Jesus came from Nazareth in the province of Galilee, and was baptized by John in the Jordan. ¹⁰ As soon as Jesus came up out of the water, he saw heaven opening and the Spirit coming down on him like a dove. ¹¹ And a voice came from heaven, "You are my own dear Son. I am pleased with you."

¹² At once the Spirit made him go into the desert, ¹³ where he stayed 40 days, being tempted by Satan. Wild animals were there also, but angels came and helped him.

Jesus Calls Four Fishermen

¹⁴ After John had been put in prison, Jesus went to Galilee and preached the Good News from God. ¹⁵ "The right time has come," he said, "and the Kingdom of God is near! Turn away from your sins and believe the Good News!"

[16] As Jesus walked along the shore of Lake Galilee, he saw two fishermen, Simon and his brother Andrew, catching fish with a net. [17] Jesus said to them, "Come with me, and I will teach you to catch people." [18] At once they left their nets and went with him.

[19] He went a little farther on and saw two other brothers, James and John, the sons of Zebedee. They were in their boat getting their nets ready. [20] As soon as Jesus saw them, he called them; they left their father Zebedee in the boat with the hired men and went with Jesus.

A Man with an Evil Spirit

[21] Jesus and his disciples came to the town of Capernaum, and on the next Sabbath Jesus went to the synagogue and began to teach. [22] The people who heard him were amazed at the way he taught, for he wasn't like the teachers of the Law; instead, he taught with authority.

[23] Just then a man with an evil spirit in him came into the synagogue and screamed, [24] "What do you want with us, Jesus of Nazareth? Are you here to destroy us? I know who you are – you are God's holy messenger!"

[25] Jesus ordered the spirit, "Be quiet, and come out of the man!"

[26] The evil spirit shook the man hard, gave a loud scream, and came out of him. [27] The people were all so amazed that they started saying to one another, "What is

this? Is it some kind of new teaching? This man has authority to give orders to the evil spirits, and they obey him!"

²⁸ And so the news about Jesus spread quickly everywhere in the province of Galilee.

Jesus Heals Many People

²⁹ Jesus and his disciples, including James and John, left the synagogue and went straight to the home of Simon and Andrew. ³⁰ Simon's mother-in-law was sick in bed with a fever, and as soon as Jesus arrived, he was told about her. ³¹ He went to her, took her by the hand, and helped her up. The fever left her, and she began to wait on them.

³² After the sun had set and evening had come, people brought to Jesus all the sick and those who had demons. ³³ All the people of the town gathered in front of the house. ³⁴ Jesus healed many who were sick with all kinds of diseases and drove out many demons. He would not let the demons say anything, because they knew who he was.

Jesus Preaches in Galilee

³⁵ Very early the next morning, long before daylight, Jesus got up and left the house. He went out of the town to a lonely place, where he prayed. ³⁶ But Simon and his companions went out searching for him, ³⁷ and when they found him, they said, "Everyone is looking for you."

³⁸ But Jesus answered, "We must go on to the other

villages round here. I have to preach in them also, because that is why I came."

³⁹ So he travelled all over Galilee, preaching in the synagogues and driving out demons.

Jesus Heals a Man

⁴⁰ A man suffering from a dreaded skin disease came to Jesus, knelt down, and begged him for help. "If you want to," he said, "you can make me clean."ᵃ

⁴¹ Jesus was filled with pity,ᵇ and stretched out his hand and touched him. "I do want to," he answered. "Be clean!" ⁴² At once the disease left the man, and he was clean. ⁴³ Then Jesus spoke sternly to him and sent him away at once, ⁴⁴ after saying to him, "Listen, don't tell anyone about this. But go straight to the priest and let him examine you; then in order to prove to everyone that you are cured, offer the sacrifice that Moses ordered."

⁴⁵ But the man went away and began to spread the news everywhere. Indeed, he talked so much that Jesus could not go into a town publicly. Instead, he stayed out in lonely places, and people came to him from everywhere.

a. 1.40 MAKE ME CLEAN: *This disease was considered to make a person ritually unclean.*
b. 1.41 pity; *some manuscripts have* anger.

Jesus Heals a Paralysed Man

2 A few days later Jesus went back to Capernaum, and the news spread that he was at home. ² So many people came together that there was no room left, not even out in front of the door. Jesus was preaching the message to them ³ when four men arrived, carrying a paralysed man to Jesus. ⁴ Because of the crowd, however, they could not get the man to him. So they made a hole in the roof right above the place where Jesus was. When they had made an opening, they let the man down, lying on his mat. ⁵ Seeing how much faith they had, Jesus said to the paralysed man, "My son, your sins are forgiven."

⁶ Some teachers of the Law who were sitting there thought to themselves, ⁷ "How does he dare to talk like this? This is blasphemy! God is the only one who can forgive sins!"

⁸ At once Jesus knew what they were thinking, so he said to them, "Why do you think such things? ⁹ Is it easier to say to this paralysed man, 'Your sins are forgiven', or to say, 'Get up, pick up your mat, and walk'? ¹⁰ I will prove to you, then, that the Son of Man has authority on earth to forgive sins." So he said to the paralysed man, ¹¹ "I tell you, get up, pick up your mat, and go home!"

¹² While they all watched, the man got up, picked up his mat, and hurried away. They were all completely

amazed and praised God, saying, "We have never seen anything like this!"

Jesus Calls Levi

[13] Jesus went back again to the shore of Lake Galilee. A crowd came to him, and he started teaching them. [14] As he walked along, he saw a tax collector, Levi son of Alphaeus, sitting in his office. Jesus said to him, "Follow me." Levi got up and followed him.

[15] Later on Jesus was having a meal in Levi's house.[a] A large number of tax collectors and other outcasts were following Jesus, and many of them joined him and his disciples at the table. [16] Some teachers of the Law, who were Pharisees, saw that Jesus was eating with these outcasts and tax collectors, so they asked his disciples, "Why does he eat with such people?"

[17] Jesus heard them and answered, "People who are well do not need a doctor, but only those who are sick. I have not come to call respectable people, but outcasts."

The Question about Fasting

[18] On one occasion the followers of John the Baptist and the Pharisees were fasting. Some people came to Jesus and asked him, "Why is it that the disciples of John

a. 2.15 in Levi's house; *or* in his (*that is,* Jesus') house.

the Baptist and the disciples of the Pharisees fast, but yours do not?"

¹⁹ Jesus answered, "Do you expect the guests at a wedding party to go without food? Of course not! As long as the bridegroom is with them, they will not do that. ²⁰ But the day will come when the bridegroom will be taken away from them, and then they will fast.

²¹ "No one uses a piece of new cloth to patch up an old coat, because the new patch will shrink and tear off some of the old cloth, making an even bigger hole. ²² Nor does anyone pour new wine into used wineskins, because the wine will burst the skins, and both the wine and the skins will be ruined. Instead, new wine must be poured into fresh wineskins."

The Question about the Sabbath

²³ Jesus was walking through some cornfields on the Sabbath. As his disciples walked along with him, they began to pick the ears of corn. ²⁴ So the Pharisees said to Jesus, "Look, it is against our Law for your disciples to do that on the Sabbath!"

²⁵ Jesus answered, "Have you never read what David did that time when he needed something to eat? He and his men were hungry, ²⁶ so he went into the house of God and ate the bread offered to God. This happened when Abiathar was the High Priest. According to our Law only

the priests may eat this bread – but David ate it and even gave it to his men."

²⁷ And Jesus concluded, "The Sabbath was made for the good of human beings; they were not made for the Sabbath. ²⁸ So the Son of Man is Lord even of the Sabbath."

The Man with a Paralysed Hand

3 Then Jesus went back to the synagogue, where there was a man who had a paralysed hand. ² Some people were there who wanted to accuse Jesus of doing wrong; so they watched him closely to see whether he would heal the man on the Sabbath. ³ Jesus said to the man, "Come up here to the front." ⁴ Then he asked the people, "What does our Law allow us to do on the Sabbath? To help or to harm? To save someone's life or to destroy it?"

But they did not say a thing. ⁵ Jesus was angry as he looked round at them, but at the same time he felt sorry for them, because they were so stubborn and wrong. Then he said to the man, "Stretch out your hand." He stretched it out, and it became well again. ⁶ So the Pharisees left the synagogue and met at once with some members of Herod's party, and they made plans to kill Jesus.

A Crowd by the Lake

[7] Jesus and his disciples went away to Lake Galilee, and a large crowd followed him. They had come from Galilee, from Judea, [8] from Jerusalem, from the territory of Idumea, from the territory on the east side of the Jordan, and from the region round the cities of Tyre and Sidon. All these people came to Jesus because they had heard of the things he was doing. [9] The crowd was so large that Jesus told his disciples to get a boat ready for him, so that the people would not crush him. [10] He had healed many people, and all those who were ill kept pushing their way to him in order to touch him. [11] And whenever the people who had evil spirits in them saw him, they would fall down before him and scream, "You are the Son of God!"

[12] Jesus sternly ordered the evil spirits not to tell anyone who he was.

Jesus Chooses the Twelve Apostles

[13] Then Jesus went up a hill and called to himself the men he wanted. They came to him, [14] and he chose twelve, whom he named apostles. "I have chosen you to be with me," he told them. "I will also send you out to preach, [15] and you will have authority to drive out demons."

[16] These are the twelve he chose: Simon (Jesus gave

him the name Peter); [17] James and his brother John, the sons of Zebedee (Jesus gave them the name Boanerges, which means "Men of Thunder"); [18] Andrew, Philip, Bartholomew, Matthew, Thomas, James son of Alphaeus, Thaddaeus, Simon the Patriot, [19] and Judas Iscariot, who betrayed Jesus.

Jesus and Beelzebul

[20] Then Jesus went home. Again such a large crowd gathered that Jesus and his disciples had no time to eat. [21] When his family heard about it, they set out to take charge of him, because people were saying, "He's gone mad!"

[22] Some teachers of the Law who had come from Jerusalem were saying, "He has Beelzebul in him! It is the chief of the demons who gives him the power to drive them out."

[23] So Jesus called them to him and spoke to them in parables: "How can Satan drive out Satan? [24] If a country divides itself into groups which fight each other, that country will fall apart. [25] If a family divides itself into groups which fight each other, that family will fall apart. [26] So if Satan's kingdom divides into groups, it cannot last, but will fall apart and come to an end.

[27] "No one can break into a strong man's house and take away his belongings unless he first ties up the strong man; then he can plunder his house.

²⁸ "I assure you that people can be forgiven all their sins and all the evil things they may say. ᵃ ²⁹ But whoever says evil things against the Holy Spirit will never be forgiven, because he has committed an eternal sin." ³⁰ (Jesus said this because some people were saying, "He has an evil spirit in him.")

Jesus' Mother and Brothers

³¹ Then Jesus' mother and brothers arrived. They stood outside the house and sent in a message, asking for him. ³² A crowd was sitting round Jesus, and they said to him, "Look, your mother and your brothers and sisters are outside, and they want you."

³³ Jesus answered, "Who is my mother? Who are my brothers?" ³⁴ He looked at the people sitting round him and said, "Look! Here are my mother and my brothers! ³⁵ Whoever does what God wants him to do is my brother, my sister, my mother."

The Parable of the Sower

4 Again Jesus began to teach beside Lake Galilee. The crowd that gathered round him was so large that he got into a boat and sat in it. The boat was out in the

---

a 3.28 evil things they may say; *or* evil things they may say against God.

water, and the crowd stood on the shore at the water's edge. [2] He used parables to teach them many things, saying to them:

[3] "Listen! Once there was a man who went out to sow corn. [4] As he scattered the seed in the field, some of it fell along the path, and the birds came and ate it up. [5] Some of it fell on rocky ground, where there was little soil. The seeds soon sprouted, because the soil wasn't deep. [6] Then, when the sun came up, it burnt the young plants; and because the roots had not grown deep enough, the plants soon dried up. [7] Some of the seed fell among thorn bushes, which grew up and choked the plants, and they didn't produce any corn. [8] But some seeds fell in good soil, and the plants sprouted, grew, and produced corn: some had thirty grains, others sixty, and others a hundred."

[9] And Jesus concluded, "Listen, then, if you have ears!"

The Purpose of the Parables

[10] When Jesus was alone, some of those who had heard him came to him with the twelve disciples and asked him to explain the parables. [11] "You have been given the secret of the Kingdom of God," Jesus answered. "But the others, who are on the outside, hear all things by means of parables, [12] so that,

'They may look and look,
    yet not see;

they may listen and listen,
    yet not understand.
For if they did, they would turn to God,
    and he would forgive them.' "

Jesus Explains the Parable of the Sower

[13] Then Jesus asked them, "Don't you understand this parable? How, then, will you ever understand any parable? [14] The sower sows God's message. [15] Some people are like the seeds that fall along the path; as soon as they hear the message, Satan comes and takes it away. [16] Other people are like the seeds that fall on rocky ground. As soon as they hear the message, they receive it gladly. [17] But it does not sink deep into them, and they don't last long. So when trouble or persecution comes because of the message, they give up at once. [18] Other people are like the seeds sown among the thorn bushes. These are the ones who hear the message, [19] but the worries about this life, the love for riches, and all other kinds of desires crowd in and choke the message, and they don't bear fruit. [20] But other people are like the seeds sown in good soil. They hear the message, accept it, and bear fruit: some thirty, some sixty, and some a hundred."

A Lamp under a Bowl

[21] Jesus continued, "Does anyone ever bring in a lamp and put it under a bowl or under the bed? Doesn't he put

it on the lampstand? [22] Whatever is hidden away will be brought out into the open, and whatever is covered up will be uncovered. [23] Listen, then, if you have ears!"

[24] He also said to them, "Pay attention to what you hear! The same rules you use to judge others will be used by God to judge you – but with even greater severity. [25] Those who have something will be given more, and those who have nothing will have taken away from them even the little they have."

The Parable of the Growing Seed

[26] Jesus went on to say, "The Kingdom of God is like this. A man scatters seed in his field.[27] He sleeps at night, is up and about during the day, and all the while the seeds are sprouting and growing. Yet he does not know how it happens. [28] The soil itself makes the plants grow and bear fruit; first the tender stalk appears, then the ear, and finally the ear full of corn. [29] When the corn is ripe, the man starts cutting it with his sickle, because harvest time has come.

The Parable of the Mustard Seed

[30] "What shall we say the Kingdom of God is like?" asked Jesus. "What parable shall we use to explain it? [31] It is like this. A man takes a mustard seed, the smallest seed in the world, and plants it in the ground. [32] After a while

it grows up and becomes the biggest of all plants. It puts out such large branches that the birds come and make their nests in its shade."

³³ Jesus preached his message to the people, using many other parables like these; he told them as much as they could understand. ³⁴ He would not speak to them without using parables, but when he was alone with his disciples, he would explain everything to them.

Jesus Calms a Storm

³⁵ On the evening of that same day Jesus said to his disciples, "Let us go across to the other side of the lake." ³⁶ So they left the crowd; the disciples got into the boat in which Jesus was already sitting, and they took him with them. Other boats were there too. ³⁷ Suddenly a strong wind blew up, and the waves began to spill over into the boat, so that it was about to fill with water. ³⁸ Jesus was in the back of the boat, sleeping with his head on a pillow. The disciples woke him up and said, "Teacher, don't you care that we are about to die?"

³⁹ Jesus stood up and commanded the wind, "Be quiet!" and he said to the waves, "Be still!" The wind died down, and there was a great calm. ⁴⁰ Then Jesus said to his disciples, "Why are you frightened? Have you still no faith?"

⁴¹ But they were terribly afraid and said to one another, "Who is this man? Even the wind and the waves obey him!"

Jesus Heals a Man with Evil Spirits

5 Jesus and his disciples arrived on the other side of Lake Galilee, in the territory of Gerasa. ² As soon as Jesus got out of the boat, he was met by a man who came out of the burial caves there. This man had an evil spirit in him ³ and lived among the tombs. Nobody could keep him chained up any more; ⁴ many times his feet and hands had been chained, but every time he broke the chains and smashed the irons on his feet. He was too strong for anyone to control him. ⁵ Day and night he wandered among the tombs and through the hills, screaming and cutting himself with stones.

⁶ He was some distance away when he saw Jesus; so he ran, fell on his knees before him, ⁷ and screamed in a loud voice, "Jesus, Son of the Most High God! What do you want with me? For God's sake, I beg you, don't punish me!" ⁸ (He said this because Jesus was saying, "Evil spirit, come out of this man!")

⁹ So Jesus asked him, "What is your name?"

The man answered, "My name is 'Mob' – there are so many of us!" ¹⁰ And he kept begging Jesus not to send the evil spirits out of that region.

¹¹ There was a large herd of pigs near by, feeding on a hillside. ¹² So the spirits begged Jesus, "Send us to the pigs, and let us go into them." ¹³ He let them go, and the evil spirits went out of the man and entered the pigs.

The whole herd – about 2,000 pigs in all – rushed down the side of the cliff into the lake and was drowned.

¹⁴ The men who had been taking care of the pigs ran away and spread the news in the town and among the farms. People went out to see what had happened, ¹⁵ and when they came to Jesus, they saw the man who used to have the mob of demons in him. He was sitting there, clothed and in his right mind; and they were all afraid. ¹⁶ Those who had seen it told the people what had happened to the man with the demons, and about the pigs.

¹⁷ So they asked Jesus to leave their territory.

¹⁸ As Jesus was getting into the boat, the man who had had the demons begged him, "Let me go with you!"

¹⁹ But Jesus would not let him. Instead, he told him, "Go back home to your family and tell them how much the Lord has done for you and how kind he has been to you."

²⁰ So the man left and went all through the Ten Towns, telling what Jesus had done for him. And all who heard it were amazed.

Jairus' Daughter and the Woman who Touched Jesus' Cloak

²¹ Jesus went back across to the other side of the lake. There at the lakeside a large crowd gathered round him.

²² Jairus, an official of the local synagogue, arrived, and when he saw Jesus, he threw himself down at his feet ²³ and begged him earnestly, "My little daughter is very ill. Please come and place your hands on her, so that she will get well and live!"

²⁴ Then Jesus started off with him. So many people were going along with Jesus that they were crowding him from every side.

²⁵ There was a woman who had suffered terribly from severe bleeding for twelve years, ²⁶ even though she had been treated by many doctors. She had spent all her money, but instead of getting better she got worse all the time. ²⁷ She had heard about Jesus, so she came in the crowd behind him, ²⁸ saying to herself, "If I just touch his clothes, I will get well."

²⁹ She touched his cloak, and her bleeding stopped at once; and she had the feeling inside herself that she was healed of her trouble. ³⁰ At once Jesus knew that power had gone out of him, so he turned round in the crowd and asked, "Who touched my clothes?"

³¹ His disciples answered, "You see how the people are crowding you; why do you ask who touched you?"

³² But Jesus kept looking round to see who had done it. ³³ The woman realized what had happened to her, so she came, trembling with fear, knelt at his feet, and told him the whole truth. ³⁴ Jesus said to her, "My daughter,

your faith has made you well. Go in peace, and be healed of your trouble."

[35] While Jesus was saying this, some messengers came from Jairus' house and told him, "Your daughter has died. Why bother the Teacher any longer?"

[36] Jesus paid no attention to [a] what they said, but told him, "Don't be afraid, only believe." [37] Then he did not let anyone else go on with him except Peter and James and his brother John. [38] They arrived at Jairus' house, where Jesus saw the confusion and heard all the loud crying and wailing. [39] He went in and said to them, "Why all this confusion? Why are you crying? The child is not dead – she is only sleeping!"

[40] They laughed at him, so he put them all out, took the child's father and mother and his three disciples, and went into the room where the child was lying. [41] He took her by the hand and said to her, "*Talitha, koum*," which means, "Little girl, I tell you to get up!"

[42] She got up at once and started walking around. (She was twelve years old.) When this happened, they were completely amazed. [43] But Jesus gave them strict orders not to tell anyone, and he said, "Give her something to eat."

a 5.36 paid no attention to; *or* overheard.

Jesus is Rejected at Nazareth

6 Jesus left that place and went back to his home town, followed by his disciples. [2] On the Sabbath he began to teach in the synagogue. Many people were there; and when they heard him, they were all amazed. "Where did he get all this?" they asked. "What wisdom is this that has been given him? How does he perform miracles? [3] Isn't he the carpenter, the son of Mary, and the brother of James, Joseph, Judas, and Simon? Aren't his sisters living here?" And so they rejected him.

[4] Jesus said to them, "Prophets are respected everywhere except in their own home town and by their relatives and their family."

[5] He was not able to perform any miracles there, except that he placed his hands on a few sick people and healed them. [6] He was greatly surprised, because the people did not have faith.

Jesus Sends out the Twelve Disciples

Then Jesus went to the villages round there, teaching the people. [7] He called the twelve disciples together and sent them out two by two. He gave them authority over the evil spirits [8] and ordered them, "Don't take anything with you on your journey except a stick – no bread, no beggar's bag, no money in your pockets. [9] Wear sandals, but don't carry an extra shirt." [10] He also said, "Wherever you are

welcomed, stay in the same house until you leave that place.
[11] If you come to a town where people do not welcome you
or will not listen to you, leave it and shake the dust off your
feet. That will be a warning to them!"

[12] So they went out and preached that people should
turn away from their sins. [13] They drove out many demons,
and rubbed olive oil on many sick people and healed them.

The Death of John the Baptist

[14] Now King Herod [a] heard about all this, because
Jesus' reputation had spread everywhere. Some people
were saying, "John the Baptist has come back to life! That
is why he has this power to perform miracles."

[15] Others, however, said, "He is Elijah."

Others said, "He is a prophet, like one of the prophets
of long ago."

[16] When Herod heard it, he said, "He is John the
Baptist! I had his head cut off, but he has come back to
life!" [17] Herod himself had ordered John's arrest, and
he had him chained and put in prison. Herod did this
because of Herodias, whom he had married, even though
she was the wife of his brother Philip. [18] John the Baptist
kept telling Herod, "It isn't right for you to be married to
your brother's wife!"

a 6.14 KING HEROD: *Herod Antipas, ruler of Galilee.*

¹⁹ So Herodias held a grudge against John and wanted to kill him, but she could not because of Herod. ²⁰ Herod was afraid of John because he knew that John was a good and holy man, and so he kept him safe. He liked to listen to him, even though he became greatly disturbed every time he heard him.

²¹ Finally Herodias got her chance. It was on Herod's birthday, when he gave a feast for all the chief government officials, the military commanders, and the leading citizens of Galilee. ²² The daughter of Herodias ᵃ came in and danced, and pleased Herod and his guests. So the king said to the girl, "What would you like to have? I will give you anything you want." ²³ With many vows he said to her, "I swear that I will give you anything you ask for, even as much as half my kingdom!"

²⁴ So the girl went out and asked her mother, "What shall I ask for?"

"The head of John the Baptist," she answered.

²⁵ The girl hurried back at once to the king and demanded, "I want you to give me here and now the head of John the Baptist on a dish!"

²⁶ This made the king very sad, but he could not refuse her because of the vows he had made in front of all his

---

a 6.22 The daughter of Herodias; *some manuscripts have* His daughter Herodias.

guests. [27] So he sent off a guard at once with orders to bring John's head. The guard left, went to the prison, and cut John's head off; [28] then he brought it on a dish and gave it to the girl, who gave it to her mother. [29] When John's disciples heard about this, they came and took away his body, and buried it.

Jesus Feeds a Great Crowd

[30] The apostles returned and met with Jesus, and told him all they had done and taught. [31] There were so many people coming and going that Jesus and his disciples didn't even have time to eat. So he said to them, "Let us go off by ourselves to some place where we will be alone and you can rest for a while." [32] So they started out in a boat by themselves for a lonely place.

[33] Many people, however, saw them leave and knew at once who they were; so they went from all the towns and ran ahead by land and arrived at the place ahead of Jesus and his disciples. [34] When Jesus got out of the boat, he saw this large crowd, and his heart was filled with pity for them, because they were like sheep without a shepherd. So he began to teach them many things. [35] When it was getting late, his disciples came to him and said, "It is already very late, and this is a lonely place. [36] Send the people away, and let them go to the nearby farms and villages in order to buy themselves something to eat."

[37] "You yourselves give them something to eat," Jesus answered.

They asked, "Do you want us to go and spend two hundred silver coins [a] on bread in order to feed them?"

[38] So Jesus asked them, "How much bread have you got? Go and see."

When they found out, they told him, "Five loaves and also two fish."

[39] Jesus then told his disciples to make all the people divide into groups and sit down on the green grass. [40] So the people sat down in rows, in groups of a hundred and groups of fifty. [41] Then Jesus took the five loaves and the two fish, looked up to heaven, and gave thanks to God. He broke the loaves and gave them to his disciples to distribute to the people. He also divided the two fish among them all. [42] Everyone ate and had enough. [43] Then the disciples took up twelve baskets full of what was left of the bread and the fish. [44] The number of men who were fed was 5,000.

Jesus Walks on the Water

[45] At once Jesus made his disciples get into the boat and go ahead of him to Bethsaida, on the other side of

a 6.37 SILVER COINS: *A silver coin was the daily wage of a rural worker (see Mt 20.2).*

the lake, while he sent the crowd away. ⁴⁶ After saying goodbye to the people he went away to a hill to pray. ⁴⁷ When evening came, the boat was in the middle of the lake, while Jesus was alone on land. ⁴⁸ He saw that his disciples were straining at the oars, because they were rowing against the wind; so some time between three and six o'clock in the morning he came to them, walking on the water. He was going to pass them by, ᵃ ⁴⁹ but they saw him walking on the water. "It's a ghost!" they thought, and screamed. ⁵⁰ They were all terrified when they saw him.

Jesus spoke to them at once, "Courage!" he said. "It is I. Don't be afraid!" ⁵¹ Then he got into the boat with them, and the wind died down. The disciples were completely amazed, ⁵² because they had not understood the real meaning of the feeding of the 5,000; their minds could not grasp it.

Jesus Heals the Sick in Gennesaret

⁵³ They crossed the lake and came to land at Gennesaret, where they tied up the boat. ⁵⁴ As they left the boat, people recognized Jesus at once. ⁵⁵ So they ran throughout the whole region; and wherever they heard he was, they brought to him sick people lying on their mats. ⁵⁶ And everywhere Jesus went, to villages, towns, or farms,

a 6.48 pass them by; *or* join them.

people would take those who were ill to the market places and beg him to let them at least touch the edge of his cloak; and all who touched it were made well.

The Teaching of the Ancestors

7 Some Pharisees and teachers of the Law who had come from Jerusalem gathered round Jesus. [2] They noticed that some of his disciples were eating their food with hands that were ritually unclean – that is, they had not washed them in the way the Pharisees said people should.

[3] (For the Pharisees, as well as the rest of the Jews, follow the teaching they received from their ancestors: they do not eat unless they wash their hands in the proper way; [4] nor do they eat anything that comes from the market unless they wash it first. [a] And they follow many other rules which they have received, such as the proper way to wash cups, pots, copper bowls, and beds. [b])

[5] So the Pharisees and the teachers of the Law asked Jesus, "Why is it that your disciples do not follow the teaching handed down by our ancestors, but instead eat with ritually unclean hands?"

a 7.4 *anything that comes from the market unless they wash it first; or anything after they come from the market unless they wash themselves first.*

b 7.4 *Some manuscripts do not have* and beds.

⁶ Jesus answered them, "How right Isaiah was when he prophesied about you! You are hypocrites, just as he wrote:

'These people, says God, honour me with their words,
    but their heart is really far away from me.
⁷ It is no use for them to worship me,
    because they teach human rules
    as though they were God's laws!'

⁸ "You put aside God's command and obey human teachings."

⁹ And Jesus continued, "You have a clever way of rejecting God's law in order to uphold your own teaching. ¹⁰ For Moses commanded, 'Respect your father and your mother,' and, 'Whoever curses his father or his mother is to be put to death.' ¹¹ But you teach that if a person has something he could use to help his father or mother, but says, 'This is Corban' (which means, it belongs to God), ¹² he is excused from helping his father or mother. ¹³ In this way the teaching you pass on to others cancels out the word of God. And there are many other things like this that you do."

The Things that Make a Person Unclean

¹⁴ Then Jesus called the crowd to him once more and said to them, "Listen to me, all of you, and understand. ¹⁵ There is nothing that goes into a person from the

outside which can make him ritually unclean. Rather, it is what comes out of a person that makes him unclean."[a]

[17] When he left the crowd and went into the house, his disciples asked him to explain this saying. [18] "You are no more intelligent than the others," Jesus said to them. "Don't you understand? Nothing that goes into a person from the outside can really make him unclean, [19] because it does not go into his heart but into his stomach and then goes on out of the body." (In saying this, Jesus declared that all foods are fit to be eaten.)

[20] And he went on to say, "It is what comes out of a person that makes him unclean. [21] For from the inside, from a person's heart, come the evil ideas which lead him to do immoral things, to rob, kill, [22] commit adultery, be greedy, and do all sorts of evil things; deceit, indecency, jealousy, slander, pride, and folly – [23] all these evil things come from inside a person and make him unclean."

A Woman's Faith

[24] Then Jesus left and went away to the territory near the city of Tyre. He went into a house and did not want anyone to know he was there, but he could not stay hidden. [25] A woman, whose daughter had an evil spirit in

a 7.15 *Some manuscripts add verse 16:* Listen, then, if you have ears! (*see 4.23*).

her, heard about Jesus and came to him at once and fell at his feet. ²⁶ The woman was a Gentile, born in the region of Phoenicia in Syria. She begged Jesus to drive the demon out of her daughter. ²⁷ But Jesus answered, "Let us first feed the children. It isn't right to take the children's food and throw it to the dogs."

²⁸ "Sir," she answered, "even the dogs under the table eat the children's leftovers!"

²⁹ So Jesus said to her, "Because of that answer, go back home, where you will find that the demon has gone out of your daughter!"

³⁰ She went home and found her child lying on the bed; the demon had indeed gone out of her.

Jesus Heals a Deaf-mute

³¹ Jesus then left the neighbourhood of Tyre and went on through Sidon to Lake Galilee, going by way of the territory of the Ten Towns. ³² Some people brought him a man who was deaf and could hardly speak, and they begged Jesus to place his hands on him. ³³ So Jesus took him off alone, away from the crowd, put his fingers in the man's ears, spat, and touched the man's tongue. ³⁴ Then Jesus looked up to heaven, gave a deep groan, and said to the man, "*Ephphatha*," which means, "Open up!"

³⁵ At once the man was able to hear, his speech impediment was removed, and he began to talk without any

trouble. 36 Then Jesus ordered the people not to speak of it to anyone; but the more he ordered them not to, the more they spoke. 37 And all who heard were completely amazed. "How well he does everything!" they exclaimed. "He even causes the deaf to hear and the dumb to speak!"

Jesus Feeds Four Thousand People

8 Not long afterwards another large crowd came together. When the people had nothing left to eat, Jesus called the disciples to him and said, 2 "I feel sorry for these people, because they have been with me for three days and now have nothing to eat. 3 If I send them home without feeding them, they will faint as they go, because some of them have come a long way."

4 His disciples asked him, "Where in this desert can anyone find enough food to feed all these people?"

5 How much bread have you got?" Jesus asked.

"Seven loaves," they answered.

6 He ordered the crowd to sit down on the ground. Then he took the seven loaves, gave thanks to God, broke them, and gave them to his disciples to distribute to the crowd; and the disciples did so. 7 They also had a few small fish. Jesus gave thanks for these and told the disciples to distribute them too. 8-9 Everybody ate and had enough — there were about 4,000 people. Then the disciples took up seven baskets full of pieces left over.

Jesus sent the people away [10] and at once got into a boat with his disciples and went to the district of Dalmanutha.

The Pharisees Ask for a Miracle

[11] Some Pharisees came to Jesus and started to argue with him. They wanted to trap him, so they asked him to perform a miracle to show that God approved of him. [12] But Jesus gave a deep groan and said, "Why do the people of this day ask for a miracle? No, I tell you! No such proof will be given to these people!"

[13] He left them, got back into the boat, and started across to the other side of the lake.

The Yeast of the Pharisees and of Herod

[14] The disciples had forgotten to bring enough bread and had only one loaf with them in the boat. [15] "Take care," Jesus warned them, "and be on your guard against the yeast of the Pharisees and the yeast of Herod."

[16] They started discussing among themselves: "He says this because we haven't any bread."

[17] Jesus knew what they were saying, so he asked them, "Why are you discussing about not having any bread? Don't you know or understand yet? Are your minds so dull? [18] You have eyes – can't you see? You have ears – can't you hear? Don't you remember [19] when I broke the five

loaves for the five thousand people? How many baskets full of leftover pieces did you take up?"

"Twelve," they answered.

[20] "And when I broke the seven loaves for the four thousand people," asked Jesus, "how many baskets full of leftover pieces did you take up?"

"Seven," they answered.

[21] "And you still don't understand?" he asked them.

Jesus Heals a Blind Man at Bethsaida

[22] They came to Bethsaida, where some people brought a blind man to Jesus and begged him to touch him. [23] Jesus took the blind man by the hand and led him out of the village. After spitting on the man's eyes, Jesus placed his hands on him and asked him, "Can you see anything?"

[24] The man looked up and said, "Yes, I can see people, but they look like trees walking about."

[25] Jesus again placed his hands on the man's eyes. This time the man looked intently, his eyesight returned, and he saw everything clearly. [26] Jesus then sent him home with the order, "Don't go back into the village."

Peter's Declaration about Jesus

[27] Then Jesus and his disciples went away to the villages near Caesarea Philippi. On the way he asked them,

"Tell me, who do people say I am?"

²⁸ Some say that you are John the Baptist," they answered; "others say that you are Elijah, while others say that you are one of the prophets."

²⁹ "What about you?" he asked them. "Who do you say I am?"

Peter answered, "You are the Messiah."

³⁰ Then Jesus ordered them, "Do not tell anyone about me."

Jesus Speaks about his Suffering and Death

³¹ Then Jesus began to teach his disciples: "The Son of Man must suffer much and be rejected by the elders, the chief priests, and the teachers of the Law. He will be put to death, but three days later he will rise to life." ³² He made this very clear to them. So Peter took him aside and began to rebuke him. ³³ But Jesus turned round, looked at his disciples, and rebuked Peter. "Get away from me, Satan," he said. "Your thoughts don't come from God but from human nature!"

³⁴ Then Jesus called the crowd and his disciples to him. "If anyone wants to come with me," he told them, "he must forget self, carry his cross, and follow me. ³⁵ For whoever wants to save his own life will lose it; but whoever loses his life for me and for the gospel will save it.

[36] Do people gain anything if they win the whole world but lose their life? Of course not! [37] There is nothing they can give to regain their life. [38] If a person is ashamed of me and of my teaching in this godless and wicked day, then the Son of Man will be ashamed of him when he comes in the glory of his Father with the holy angels."

9 And he went on to say, "I tell you, there are some here who will not die until they have seen the Kingdom of God come with power."

The Transfiguration

[2] Six days later Jesus took with him Peter, James and John, and led them up a high mountain, where they were alone. As they looked on, a change came over Jesus, [3] and his clothes became shining white – whiter than anyone in the world could wash them. [4] Then the three disciples saw Elijah and Moses talking with Jesus. [5] Peter spoke up and said to Jesus, "Teacher, how good it is that we are here! We will make three tents, one for you, one for Moses, and one for Elijah." [6] He and the others were so frightened that he did not know what to say.

[7] Then a cloud appeared and covered them with its shadow, and a voice came from the cloud, "This is my own dear Son – listen to him!" [8] They took a quick look round but did not see anyone else; only Jesus was with them.

⁹ As they came down the mountain, Jesus ordered them, "Don't tell anyone what you have seen, until the Son of Man has risen from death."

¹⁰ They obeyed his order, but among themselves they started discussing the matter, "What does this 'rising from death' mean?" ¹¹ And they asked Jesus, "Why do the teachers of the Law say that Elijah has to come first?"

¹² His answer was, "Elijah is indeed coming first in order to get everything ready. Yet why do the Scriptures say that the Son of Man will suffer much and be rejected? ¹³I tell you, however, that Elijah has already come and that people treated him just as they pleased, as the Scriptures say about him."

Jesus Heals a Boy with an Evil Spirit

¹⁴ When they joined the rest of the disciples, they saw a large crowd round them and some teachers of the Law arguing with them. ¹⁵ When the people saw Jesus, they were greatly surprised, and ran to him and greeted him. ¹⁶ Jesus asked his disciples, "What are you arguing with them about?"

¹⁷ A man in the crowd answered, "Teacher, I brought my son to you, because he has an evil spirit in him and cannot talk. ¹⁸ Whenever the spirit attacks him, it throws him to the ground, and he foams at the mouth, grits his

teeth, and becomes stiff all over. I asked your disciples to drive the spirit out, but they could not."

[19] Jesus said to them, "How unbelieving you people are! How long must I stay with you? How long do I have to put up with you? Bring the boy to me!" [20] They brought him to Jesus.

As soon as the spirit saw Jesus, it threw the boy into a fit, so that he fell on the ground and rolled round, foaming at the mouth. [21] "How long has he been like this?" Jesus asked the father.

"Ever since he was a child," he replied. [22] "Many times the evil spirit has tried to kill him by throwing him in the fire and into water. Have pity on us and help us, if you possibly can!"

[23] "Yes," said Jesus, "if you yourself can! Everything is possible for the person who has faith."

[24] The father at once cried out, "I do have faith, but not enough. Help me to have more!"

[25] Jesus noticed that the crowd was closing in on them, so he gave a command to the evil spirit. "Deaf and dumb spirit," he said, "I order you to come out of the boy and never go into him again!"

[26] The spirit screamed, threw the boy into a bad fit, and came out. The boy looked like a corpse, and everyone said, "He is dead!" [27] But Jesus took the boy by the hand and helped him to rise, and he stood up.

[28] After Jesus had gone indoors, his disciples asked him privately, "Why couldn't we drive the spirit out?"

[29] "Only prayer can drive this kind out," answered Jesus; "nothing else can."

Jesus Speaks Again about his Death

[30] Jesus and his disciples left that place and went on through Galilee. Jesus did not want anyone to know where he was, [31] because he was teaching his disciples: "The Son of Man will be handed over to those who will kill him. Three days later, however, he will rise to life."

[32] But they did not understand what this teaching meant, and they were afraid to ask him.

Who is the Greatest?

[33] They came to Capernaum, and after going indoors Jesus asked his disciples, "What were you arguing about on the road?"

[34] But they would not answer him, because on the road they had been arguing among themselves about who was the greatest. [35] Jesus sat down, called the twelve disciples, and said to them, "Whoever wants to be first must place himself last of all and be the servant of all." [36] Then he took a child and made him stand in front of them. He put his arms round him and said to them, [37] "Whoever welcomes in my name one of these children, welcomes

me; and whoever welcomes me, welcomes not only me but also the one who sent me."

Whoever is not Against Us is For Us

[38] John said to him, "Teacher, we saw a man who was driving out demons in your name, and we told him to stop, because he doesn't belong to our group."

[39] "Do not try to stop him," Jesus told them, "because no one who performs a miracle in my name will be able soon afterwards to say evil things about me. [40] For whoever is not against us is for us. [41] I assure you that anyone who gives you a drink of water because you belong to me will certainly receive his reward.

Temptations to Sin

[42] "If anyone should cause one of these little ones to lose his faith in me, it would be better for that person to have a large millstone tied round his neck and be thrown into the sea. [43] So if your hand makes you lose your faith, cut it off! It is better for you to enter life without a hand than to keep both hands and go off to hell, to the fire that never goes out. [a] [45] And if your foot makes you lose your faith, cut it off! It is better for you to enter life without a foot

---

a 9.43 *Some manuscripts add verse 44:* There 'the worms that eat them never die, and the fire that burns them is never put out' *(see verse 48).*

than to keep both feet and be thrown into hell. [b] 47 And if your eye makes you lose your faith, take it out! It is better for you to enter the Kingdom of God with only one eye than to keep both eyes and be thrown into hell. 48 There 'the worms that eat them never die, and the fire that burns them is never put out.'

49 "Everyone will be purified by fire as a sacrifice is purified by salt.

50 "Salt is good; but if it loses its saltiness, how can you make it salty again?

"Have the salt of friendship among yourselves, and live in peace with one another."

Jesus Teaches about Divorce

10 Then Jesus left that place, went to the province of Judea, and crossed the River Jordan. Crowds came flocking to him again, and he taught them, as he always did.

2 Some Pharisees came to him and tried to trap him. "Tell us," they asked, "does our Law allow a man to divorce his wife?"

3 Jesus answered with a question, "What law did Moses give you?"

b 9.45 *Some manuscripts add verse 46:* There 'the worms that eat them never die, and the fire that burns them is never put out' *(see verse 48).*

⁴ Their answer was, "Moses gave permission for a man to write a divorce notice and send his wife away."

⁵ Jesus said to them, "Moses wrote this law for you because you are so hard to teach. ⁶ But in the beginning, at the time of creation, 'God made them male and female,' as the scripture says. ⁷ 'And for this reason a man will leave his father and mother and unite with his wife,ᵃ ⁸ and the two will become one.' So they are no longer two, but one. ⁹ No human being then must separate what God has joined together."

¹⁰ When they went back into the house, the disciples asked Jesus about this matter. ¹¹ He said to them, "A man who divorces his wife and marries another woman commits adultery against his wife. ¹² In the same way, a woman who divorces her husband and marries another man commits adultery."

Jesus Blesses Little Children

¹³ Some people brought children to Jesus for him to place his hands on them, but the disciples scolded the people. ¹⁴ When Jesus noticed this, he was angry and said to his disciples, "Let the children come to me, and do not stop them, because the Kingdom of God belongs to such

a 10.7 *Some manuscripts do not have* and unite with his wife.

as these. [15] I assure you that whoever does not receive the Kingdom of God like a child will never enter it." [16] Then he took the children in his arms, placed his hands on each of them, and blessed them.

The Rich Man

[17] As Jesus was starting on his way again, a man ran up, knelt before him, and asked him, "Good Teacher, what must I do to receive eternal life?"

[18] "Why do you call me good?" Jesus asked him. "No one is good except God alone. [19] You know the commandments: 'Do not commit murder; do not commit adultery; do not steal; do not accuse anyone falsely; do not cheat; respect your father and your mother.' "

[20] "Teacher," the man said, "ever since I was young, I have obeyed all these commandments."

[21] Jesus looked straight at him with love and said, "You need only one thing. Go and sell all you have and give the money to the poor, and you will have riches in heaven; then come and follow me." [22] When the man heard this, gloom spread over his face, and he went away sad, because he was very rich.

[23] Jesus looked round at his disciples and said to them, "How hard it will be for rich people to enter the Kingdom of God!"

[24] The disciples were shocked at these words, but Jesus

went on to say, "My children, how hard it is to enter the Kingdom of God! [25] It is much harder for a rich person to enter the Kingdom of God than for a camel to go through the eye of a needle."

[26] At this the disciples were completely amazed and asked one another, "Who, then, can be saved?"

[27] Jesus looked straight at them and answered, "This is impossible for human beings, but not for God; everything is possible for God."

[28] Then Peter spoke up, "Look, we have left everything and followed you."

[29] "Yes," Jesus said to them, "and I tell you that anyone who leaves home or brothers or sisters or mother or father or children or fields for me and for the gospel, [30] will receive much more in this present age. He will receive a hundred times more houses, brothers, sisters, mothers, children and fields – and persecutions as well; and in the age to come he will receive eternal life. [31] But many who now are first will be last, and many who now are last will be first."

Jesus Speaks a Third Time about his Death

[32] Jesus and his disciples were now on the road going up to Jerusalem. Jesus was going ahead of the disciples, who were filled with alarm; the people who followed behind were afraid. Once again Jesus took the twelve

disciples aside and spoke of the things that were going to happen to him. [33] "Listen," he told them, "we are going up to Jerusalem where the Son of Man will be handed over to the chief priests and the teachers of the Law. They will condemn him to death and then hand him over to the Gentiles, [34] who will mock him, spit on him, whip him, and kill him; but three days later he will rise to life."

The Request of James and John

[35] Then James and John, the sons of Zebedee, came to Jesus. "Teacher," they said, "there is something we want you to do for us."

[36] "What is it?" Jesus asked them.

[37] They answered, "When you sit on your throne in your glorious Kingdom, we want you to let us sit with you, one at your right and one at your left."

[38] Jesus said to them, "You don't know what you are asking for. Can you drink the cup of suffering that I must drink? Can you be baptized in the way I must be baptized?"

[39] "We can," they answered.

Jesus said to them, "You will indeed drink the cup I must drink and be baptized in the way I must be baptized. [40] But I do not have the right to choose who will sit at my right and my left. It is God who will give these places to those for whom he has prepared them."

[41] When the other ten disciples heard about it, they became angry with James and John. [42] So Jesus called them all together to him and said, "You know that those who are considered rulers of the heathen have power over them, and the leaders have complete authority. [43] This, however, is not the way it is among you. If one of you wants to be great, he must be the servant of the rest; [44] and if one of you wants to be first, he must be the slave of all. [45] For even the Son of Man did not come to be served; he came to serve and to give his life to redeem many people."

Jesus Heals Blind Bartimaeus

[46] They came to Jericho, and as Jesus was leaving with his disciples and a large crowd, a blind beggar named Bartimaeus son of Timaeus was sitting by the road. [47] When he heard that it was Jesus of Nazareth, he began to shout, "Jesus! Son of David! Take pity on me!"

[48] Many of the people scolded him and told him to be quiet. But he shouted even more loudly, "Son of David, take pity on me!"

[49] Jesus stopped and said, "Call him."

So they called the blind man. "Cheer up!" they said. "Get up, he is calling you."

[50] He threw off his cloak, jumped up, and came to Jesus.

[51] "What do you want me to do for you?" Jesus asked him.

"Teacher," the blind man answered, "I want to see again."

[52] "Go," Jesus told him, "your faith has made you well."

At once he was able to see and followed Jesus on the road.

The Triumphant Entry into Jerusalem

11 As they approached Jerusalem, near the towns of Bethphage and Bethany, they came to the Mount of Olives. Jesus sent two of his disciples on ahead [2] with these instructions: "Go to the village there ahead of you. As soon as you get there, you will find a colt tied up that has never been ridden. Untie it and bring it here. [3] And if someone asks you why you are doing that, tell him that the Master [a] needs it and will send it back at once."

[4] So they went and found a colt out in the street, tied to the door of a house. As they were untying it, [5] some of the bystanders asked them, "What are you doing, untying that colt?"

[6] They answered just as Jesus had told them, and the bystanders let them go. [7] They brought the colt to Jesus, threw their cloaks over the animal, and Jesus got on.

a 11.3 the Master; *or* its owner.

[8] Many people spread their cloaks on the road, while others cut branches in the fields and spread them on the road. [9] The people who were in front and those who followed behind began to shout, "Praise God! God bless him who comes in the name of the Lord! [10] God bless the coming kingdom of King David, our father! Praise God!"

[11] Jesus entered Jerusalem, went into the Temple, and looked round at everything. But since it was already late in the day, he went out to Bethany with the twelve disciples.

Jesus Curses the Fig Tree

[12] The next day, as they were coming back from Bethany, Jesus was hungry. [13] He saw in the distance a fig tree covered with leaves, so he went to see if he could find any figs on it. But when he came to it, he found only leaves, because it was not the right time for figs. [14] Jesus said to the fig tree, "No one shall ever eat figs from you again!"

And his disciples heard him.

Jesus Goes to the Temple

[15] When they arrived in Jerusalem, Jesus went to the Temple and began to drive out all those who were buying and selling. He overturned the tables of the money-changers and the stools of those who sold pigeons, [16] and

he would not let anyone carry anything through the temple courtyards. [17] He then taught the people: "It is written in the Scriptures that God said, 'My Temple will be called a house of prayer for the people of all nations.' But you have turned it into a hideout for thieves!"

[18] The chief priests and the teachers of the Law heard of this, so they began looking for some way to kill Jesus. They were afraid of him, because the whole crowd was amazed at his teaching.

[19] When evening came, Jesus and his disciples left the city.

The Lesson from the Fig Tree

[20] Early next morning, as they walked along the road, they saw the fig tree. It was dead all the way down to its roots. [21] Peter remembered what had happened and said to Jesus, "Look, Teacher, the fig tree you cursed has died!"

[22] Jesus answered them, "Have faith in God. [23] I assure you that whoever tells this hill to get up and throw itself in the sea and does not doubt in his heart, but believes that what he says will happen, it will be done for him. [24] For this reason I tell you: when you pray and ask for something, believe that you have received it, and you will be given whatever you ask for. [25] And when you stand and pray, forgive anything you may have against anyone, so

that your Father in heaven will forgive the wrongs you have done." [a]

The Question about Jesus' Authority

[27] They arrived once again in Jerusalem. As Jesus was walking in the Temple, the chief priests, the teachers of the Law, and the elders came to him [28] and asked him, "What right have you to do these things? Who gave you this right?"

[29] Jesus answered them, "I will ask you just one question, and if you give me an answer, I will tell you what right I have to do these things. [30] Tell me, where did John's right to baptize come from: was it from God or from human beings?"

[31] They started to argue among themselves: "What shall we say? If we answer, 'From God,' he will say, 'Why, then, did you not believe John?' [32] But if we say, 'From human beings …'" (They were afraid of the people, because everyone was convinced that John had been a prophet.) [33] So their answer to Jesus, was, "We don't know."

Jesus said to them, "Neither will I tell you, then, by what right I do these things."

a 11.25 *Some manuscripts add verse 26:* If you do not forgive others, your Father in heaven will not forgive the wrongs you have done *(see Mt 6.15).*

The Parable of the Tenants in the Vineyard

12 Then Jesus spoke to them in parables: "Once there was a man who planted a vineyard, put a fence round it, dug a hole for the winepress, and built a watchtower. Then he let out the vineyard to tenants and left home on a journey. ² When the time came to gather the grapes, he sent a slave to the tenants to receive from them his share of the harvest. ³ The tenants seized the slave, beat him, and sent him back without a thing. ⁴ Then the owner sent another slave; the tenants beat him over the head and treated him shamefully. ⁵ The owner sent another slave, and they killed him; and they treated many others the same way, beating some and killing others. ⁶ The only one left to send was the man's own dear son. Last of all, then, he sent his son to the tenants. 'I am sure they will respect my son,' he said. ⁷ But those tenants said to one another, 'This is the owner's son. Come on, let's kill him, and his property will be ours!' ⁸ So they seized the son and killed him and threw his body out of the vineyard.

⁹ "What, then, will the owner of the vineyard do?" asked Jesus. "He will come and kill those tenants and hand the vineyard over to others. ¹⁰ Surely you have read this scripture:

'The stone which the builders rejected as worthless turned out to be the most important of all.

[11] This was done by the Lord;

what a wonderful sight it is!' "

[12] The Jewish leaders tried to arrest Jesus, because they knew that he had told this parable against them. But they were afraid of the crowd, so they left him and went away.

The Question about Paying Taxes

[13] Some Pharisees and some members of Herod's party were sent to Jesus to trap him with questions. [14] They came to him and said, "Teacher, we know that you tell the truth, without worrying about what people think. You pay no attention to anyone's status, but teach the truth about God's will for people. Tell us, is it against our Law to pay taxes to the Roman Emperor? Should we pay them or not?"

[15] But Jesus saw through their trick and answered, "Why are you trying to trap me? Bring a silver coin, and let me see it."

[16] They brought him one, and he asked, "Whose face and name are these?"

"The Emperor's," they answered.

[17] So Jesus said, "Well, then, pay the Emperor what belongs to the Emperor, and pay God what belongs to God."

And they were amazed at Jesus.

The Question about Rising from Death

¹⁸ Then some Sadducees, who say that people will not rise from death, came to Jesus and said, ¹⁹ "Teacher, Moses wrote this law for us: 'If a man dies and leaves a wife but no children, that man's brother must marry the widow so that they can have children who will be considered the dead man's children.' ²⁰ Once there were seven brothers; the eldest got married and died without having children. ²¹ Then the second one married the woman, and he also died without having children. The same thing happened to the third brother, ²² and then to the rest: all seven brothers married the woman and died without having children. Last of all, the woman died. ²³ Now, when all the dead rise to life on the day of resurrection, whose wife will she be? All seven of them had married her."

²⁴ Jesus answered them, "How wrong you are! And do you know why? It is because you don't know the Scriptures or God's power. ²⁵ For when the dead rise to life, they will be like the angels in heaven and will not marry. ²⁶ Now, as for the dead being raised: haven't you ever read in the Book of Moses the passage about the burning bush? There it is written that God said to Moses, 'I am the God of Abraham, the God of Isaac, and the God of Jacob.' ²⁷ He is the God of the living, not of the dead. You are completely wrong!"

The Great Commandment

[28] A teacher of the Law was there who heard the discussion. He saw that Jesus had given the Sadducees a good answer, so he came to him with a question: "Which commandment is the most important of all?"

[29] Jesus replied, "The most important one is this: 'Listen, Israel! The Lord our God is the only Lord. [a] [30] Love the Lord your God with all your heart, with all your soul, with all your mind, and with all your strength.' [31] The second most important commandment is this: 'Love your neighbour as you love yourself.' There is no other commandment more important than these two."

[32] The teacher of the Law said to Jesus, "Well done, Teacher! It is true, as you say, that only the Lord is God and that there is no other god but he. [33] And to love God with all your heart and with all your mind and with all your strength, and to love your neighbour as yourself, is more important than to offer animals and other sacrifices to God."

[34] Jesus noticed how wise his answer was, and so he told him, "You are not far from the Kingdom of God."

After this nobody dared to ask Jesus any more questions.

a 12.29 The Lord our God is the only Lord; *or* The Lord is our God, the Lord alone.

The Question about the Messiah

³⁵ As Jesus was teaching in the Temple, he asked the question, "How can the teachers of the Law say that the Messiah will be the descendant of David? ³⁶ The Holy Spirit inspired David to say:

'The Lord said to my Lord:

Sit here on my right

until I put your enemies under your feet.'

³⁷ David himself called him 'Lord'; so how can the Messiah be David's descendant?"

Jesus Warns against the Teachers of the Law

A large crowd was listening to Jesus gladly. ³⁸ As he taught them, he said, "Watch out for the teachers of the Law, who like to walk around in their long robes and be greeted with respect in the market place, ³⁹ who choose the reserved seats in the synagogues and the best places at feasts. ⁴⁰ They take advantage of widows and rob them of their homes, and then make a show of saying long prayers. Their punishment will be all the worse!"

The Widow's Offering

⁴¹ As Jesus sat near the temple treasury, he watched the people as they dropped in their money. Many rich men dropped in a lot of money; ⁴² then a poor widow came along and dropped in two little copper coins, worth

about a penny. [43] He called his disciples together and said to them, "I tell you that this poor widow put more in the offering box than all the others. [44] For the others put in what they had to spare of their riches; but she, poor as she is, put in all she had – she gave all she had to live on."

Jesus Speaks of the Destruction of the Temple

13 As Jesus was leaving the Temple, one of his disciples said, "Look, Teacher! What wonderful stones and buildings!"

[2] Jesus answered, "You see these great buildings? Not a single stone here will be left in its place; every one of them will be thrown down."

Troubles and Persecutions

[3] Jesus was sitting on the Mount of Olives, across from the Temple, when Peter, James, John, and Andrew came to him in private. [4] "Tell us when this will be," they said, "and tell us what will happen to show that the time has come for all these things to take place."

[5] Jesus said to them, "Be on guard, and don't let anyone deceive you. [6] Many men, claiming to speak for me, will come and say, 'I am he!' and they will deceive many people. [7] And don't be troubled when you hear the noise of battles close by and news of battles far away. Such things must happen, but they do not mean that the end

has come. [8] Countries will fight each other; kingdoms will attack one another. There will be earthquakes everywhere, and there will be famines. These things are like the first pains of childbirth.

[9] "You yourselves must be on guard. You will be arrested and taken to court. You will be beaten in the synagogues; you will stand before rulers and kings for my sake to tell them the Good News. [10] But before the end comes, the gospel must be preached to all peoples. [11] And when you are arrested and taken to court, do not worry beforehand about what you are going to say; when the time comes, say whatever is then given to you. For the words you speak will not be yours; they will come from the Holy Spirit. [12] Men will hand over their own brothers to be put to death, and fathers will do the same to their children. Children will turn against their parents and have them put to death. [13] Everyone will hate you because of me. But whoever holds out to the end will be saved.

The Awful Horror

[14] "You will see 'The Awful Horror' standing in the place where he should not be." (Note to the reader: be sure to understand what this means!) "Then those who are in Judea must run away to the hills. [15] Someone who is on the roof of his house must not lose time by going down into the house to get anything to take with him.

[16] Some-one who is in the field must not go back to the house for his cloak. [17] How terrible it will be in those days for women who are pregnant and for mothers with little babies! [18] Pray to God that these things will not happen in the winter! [19] For the trouble of those days will be far worse than any the world has ever known from the very beginning when God created the world until the present time. Nor will there ever be anything like it again. [20] But the Lord has reduced the number of those days; if he had not, nobody would survive. For the sake of his chosen people, however, he has reduced those days.

[21] "Then, if anyone says to you, 'Look, here is the Messiah!' or 'Look, there he is!' – do not believe him. [22] For false Messiahs and false prophets will appear. They will perform miracles and wonders in order to deceive even God's chosen people, if possible. [23] Be on your guard! I have told you everything before the time comes.

The Coming of the Son of Man

[24] "In the days after that time of trouble the sun will grow dark, the moon will no longer shine, [25] the stars will fall from heaven, and the powers in space will be driven from their courses. [26] Then the Son of Man will appear, coming in the clouds with great power and glory. [27] He will send the angels out to the four corners of the earth to gather God's chosen people from one end of the world to the other.

The Lesson of the Fig Tree

[28] "Let the fig tree teach you a lesson. When its branches become green and tender and it starts putting out leaves, you know that summer is near. [29] In the same way, when you see these things happening, you will know that the time is near, ready to begin. [a] [30] Remember that all these things will happen before the people now living have all died. [31] Heaven and earth will pass away, but my words will never pass away.

No one Knows the Day or Hour

[32] "No one knows, however, when that day or hour will come – neither the angels in heaven, nor the Son; only the Father knows. [33] Be on watch, be alert, for you do not know when the time will come. [34] It will be like a man who goes away from home on a journey and leaves his servants in charge, after giving to each one his own work to do and after telling the doorkeeper to keep watch. [35] Be on guard, then, because you do not know when the master of the house is coming – it might be in the evening or at midnight or before dawn or at sunrise. [36] If he comes suddenly, he must not find you asleep. [37] What I say to you, then, I say to all: watch!"

a 13.29 the time is near, ready to begin; *or* he is near, ready to come.

The Plot against Jesus

14 It was now two days before the Festival of Passover and Unleavened Bread. The chief priests and the teachers of the Law were looking for a way to arrest Jesus secretly and put him to death. [2] "We must not do it during the festival," they said, "or the people might riot."

Jesus is Anointed at Bethany

[3] Jesus was in Bethany at the house of Simon, a man who had suffered from a dreaded skin disease. While Jesus was eating, a woman came in with an alabaster jar full of a very expensive perfume made of pure nard. She broke the jar and poured the perfume on Jesus' head. [4] Some of the people there became angry and said to one another, "What was the use of wasting the perfume? [5] It could have been sold for more than three hundred silver coins [a] and the money given to the poor!" And they criticized her harshly.

[6] But Jesus said, "Leave her alone! Why are you bothering her? She has done a fine and beautiful thing for me. [7] You will always have poor people with you, and any time you want to, you can help them. But you will not always have me. [8] She did what she could; she poured

a 14.5 SILVER COINS: See 6.37.

perfume on my body to prepare it ahead of time for burial. [9] Now, I assure you that wherever the gospel is preached all over the world, what she has done will be told in memory of her."

Judas Agrees to Betray Jesus

[10] Then Judas Iscariot, one of the twelve disciples, went off to the chief priests in order to betray Jesus to them. [11] They were pleased to hear what he had to say, and promised to give him money. So Judas started looking for a good chance to hand Jesus over to them.

Jesus Eats the Passover Meal with his Disciples

[12] On the first day of the Festival of Unleavened Bread, the day the lambs for the Passover meal were killed, Jesus' disciples asked him, "Where do you want us to go and get the Passover meal ready for you?"

[13] Then Jesus sent two of them with these instructions: "Go into the city, and a man carrying a jar of water will meet you. Follow him [14] to the house he enters, and say to the owner of the house: 'The Teacher says, Where is the room where my disciples and I will eat the Passover meal?' [15] Then he will show you a large upstairs room, prepared and furnished, where you will get everything ready for us."

[16] The disciples left, went to the city, and found

everything just as Jesus had told them; and they prepared the Passover meal.

[17] When it was evening, Jesus came with the twelve disciples. [18] While they were at the table eating, Jesus said, "I tell you that one of you will betray me – one who is eating with me."

[19] The disciples were upset and began to ask him, one after the other, "Surely you don't mean me, do you?"

[20] Jesus answered, "It will be one of you twelve, one who dips his bread in the dish with me. [21] The Son of Man will die as the Scriptures say he will; but how terrible for that man who betrays the Son of Man! It would have been better for that man if he had never been born!"

The Lord's Supper

[22] While they were eating, Jesus took a piece of bread, gave a prayer of thanks, broke it, and gave it to his disciples. "Take it," he said, "this is my body."

[23] Then he took a cup, gave thanks to God, and handed it to them; and they all drank from it. [24] Jesus said, "This is my blood which is poured out for many, my blood which seals God's covenant. [25] I tell you, I will never again drink this wine until the day I drink the new wine in the Kingdom of God."

[26] Then they sang a hymn and went out to the Mount of Olives.

Jesus Predicts Peter's Denial

[27] Jesus said to them, "All of you will run away and leave me, for the scripture says, 'God will kill the shepherd, and the sheep will all be scattered.' [28] But after I am raised to life, I will go to Galilee ahead of you."

[29] Peter answered, "I will never leave you, even though all the rest do!"

[30] Jesus said to Peter, "I tell you that before the cock crows twice tonight, you will say three times that you do not know me."

[31] Peter answered even more strongly, "I will never say that, even if I have to die with you!"

And all the other disciples said the same thing.

Jesus Prays in Gethsemane

[32] They came to a place called Gethsemane, and Jesus said to his disciples, "Sit here while I pray." [33] He took Peter, James, and John with him. Distress and anguish came over him, [34] and he said to them, "The sorrow in my heart is so great that it almost crushes me. Stay here and keep watch."

[35] He went a little farther on, threw himself on the ground, and prayed that, if possible, he might not have to go through that time of suffering. [36] "Father," he prayed, "my Father! All things are possible for you. Take this cup of suffering away from me. Yet not what I want, but what you want."

[37] Then he returned and found the three disciples asleep. He said to Peter, "Simon, are you asleep? Weren't you able to stay awake even for one hour?" [38] And he said to them, "Keep watch, and pray that you will not fall into temptation. The spirit is willing, but the flesh is weak."

[39] He went away once more and prayed, saying the same words. [40] Then he came back to the disciples and found them asleep; they could not keep their eyes open. And they did not know what to say to him.

[41] When he came back the third time, he said to them, "Are you still sleeping and resting? Enough! The hour has come! Look, the Son of Man is now being handed over to the power of sinners. [42] Get up, let us go. Look, here is the man who is betraying me!"

The Arrest of Jesus

[43] Jesus was still speaking when Judas, one of the twelve disciples, arrived. With him was a crowd armed with swords and clubs, and sent by the chief priests, the teachers of the Law, and the elders. [44] The traitor had given the crowd a signal: "The man I kiss is the one you want. Arrest him and take him away under guard."

[45] As soon as Judas arrived, he went up to Jesus and said, "Teacher!" and kissed him. [46] So they arrested Jesus and held him tight. [47] But one of those standing there drew his sword and struck at the High Priest's slave,

cutting off his ear. [48] Then Jesus spoke up and said to them, "Did you have to come with swords and clubs to capture me, as though I were an outlaw? [49] Day after day I was with you teaching in the Temple, and you did not arrest me. But the Scriptures must come true."

[50] Then all the disciples left him and ran away.

[51] A certain young man, dressed only in a linen cloth, was following Jesus. They tried to arrest him, [52] but he ran away naked, leaving the cloth behind.

Jesus before the Council

[53] Then Jesus was taken to the High Priest's house, where all the chief priests, the elders, and the teachers of the Law were gathering. [54] Peter followed from a distance and went into the courtyard of the High Priest's house. There he sat down with the guards, keeping himself warm by the fire. [55] The chief priests and the whole Council tried to find some evidence against Jesus in order to put him to death, but they could not find any. [56] Many witnesses told lies against Jesus, but their stories did not agree.

[57] Then some men stood up and told this lie against Jesus: [58] "We heard him say, 'I will tear down this Temple which men have made, and after three days I will build one that is not made by men.' " [59] Not even they, however, could make their stories agree.

[60] The High Priest stood up in front of them all and questioned Jesus, "Have you no answer to the accusation they bring against you?"

[61] But Jesus kept quiet and would not say a word. Again the High Priest questioned him, "Are you the Messiah, the Son of the Blessed God?"

[62] "I am," answered Jesus, "and you will all see the Son of Man seated on the right of the Almighty and coming with the clouds of heaven!"

[63] The High Priest tore his robes and said, "We don't need any more witnesses! [64] You heard his blasphemy. What is your decision?"

They all voted against him: he was guilty and should be put to death.

[65] Some of them began to spit on Jesus, and they blindfolded him and hit him. "Guess who hit you!" they said. And the guards took him and slapped him.

Peter Denies Jesus

[66] Peter was still down in the courtyard when one of the High Priest's servant women came by. [67] When she saw Peter warming himself, she looked straight at him and said, "You, too, were with Jesus of Nazareth."

[68] But he denied it. "I don't know … I don't understand what you are talking about," he answered, and

went out into the passage. Just then a cock crowed. [a]

[69] The servant woman saw him there and began to repeat to the bystanders, "He is one of them!" [70] But Peter denied it again.

A little while later the bystanders accused Peter again, "You can't deny that you are one of them, because you, too, are from Galilee."

[71] Then Peter said, "I swear that I am telling the truth! May God punish me if I am not! I do not know the man you are talking about!"

[72] Just then a cock crowed a second time, and Peter remembered how Jesus had said to him, "Before the cock crows twice, you will say three times that you do not know me." And he broke down and cried.

Jesus is Brought before Pilate

15 Early in the morning the chief priests met hurriedly with the elders, the teachers of the Law, and the whole Council, and made their plans. They put Jesus in chains, led him away, and handed him over to Pilate. [2] Pilate questioned him, "Are you the king of the Jews?"

Jesus answered, "So you say."

[3] The chief priests were accusing Jesus of many things,

---

a 14.68 *Some manuscripts do not have* Just then a cock crowed.

[4] so Pilate questioned him again, "Aren't you going to answer? Listen to all their accusations!"

[5] Again Jesus refused to say a word, and Pilate was amazed.

Jesus is Sentenced to Death

[6] At every Passover Festival, Pilate was in the habit of setting free any one prisoner the people asked for. [7] At that time a man named Barabbas was in prison with the rebels who had committed murder in the riot. [8] When the crowd gathered and began to ask Pilate for the usual favour, [9] he asked them, "Do you want me to set free for you the king of the Jews?" [10] He knew very well that the chief priests had handed Jesus over to him because they were jealous.

[11] But the chief priests stirred up the crowd to ask, instead, for Pilate to set Barabbas free for them. [12] Pilate spoke again to the crowd, "What, then, do you want me to do with the one you call the king of the Jews?"

[13] They shouted back, "Crucify him!"

[14] "But what crime has he committed?" Pilate asked.

They shouted all the louder, "Crucify him!"

[15] Pilate wanted to please the crowd, so he set Barabbas free for them. Then he had Jesus whipped and handed him over to be crucified.

The Soldiers Mock Jesus

[16] The soldiers took Jesus inside to the courtyard of the governor's palace and called together the rest of the company. [17] They put a purple robe on Jesus, made a crown out of thorny branches, and put it on his head. [18] Then they began to salute him: "Long live the King of the Jews!" [19] They beat him over the head with a stick, spat on him, fell on their knees, and bowed down to him. [20] When they had finished mocking him, they took off the purple robe and put his own clothes back on him. Then they led him out to crucify him.

Jesus is Crucified

[21] On the way they met a man named Simon, who was coming into the city from the country, and the soldiers forced him to carry Jesus' cross. (Simon was from Cyrene and was the father of Alexander and Rufus.) [22] They took Jesus to a place called Golgotha, which means "The Place of the Skull". [23] There they tried to give him wine mixed with a drug called myrrh, but Jesus would not drink it. [24] Then they crucified him and divided his clothes among themselves, throwing dice to see who would get which piece of clothing. [25] It was nine o'clock in the morning when they crucified him. [26] The notice of the accusation against him said: "The King of the Jews". [27] They also

crucified two bandits with Jesus, one on his right and the other on his left. [a]

²⁹ People passing by shook their heads and hurled insults at Jesus: "Aha! You were going to tear down the Temple and build it up again in three days! ³⁰ Now come down from the cross and save yourself!"

³¹ In the same way the chief priests and the teachers of the Law jeered at Jesus, saying to each other, "He saved others, but he cannot save himself! ³² Let us see the Messiah, the king of Israel, come down from the cross now, and we will believe in him!"

And the two who were crucified with Jesus insulted him also.

The Death of Jesus

³³ At noon the whole country was covered with darkness, which lasted for three hours. ³⁴ At three o'clock Jesus cried out with a loud shout, *"Eloi, Eloi, lema sabachthani?"* which means, "My God, my God, why did you abandon me?"

³⁵ Some of the people there heard him and said, "Listen, he is calling for Elijah!" ³⁶ One of them ran up with a sponge, soaked it in cheap wine, and put it on the

---

a 15.27 *Some manuscripts add verse 28:* In this way the scripture came true which says, "He shared the fate of criminals" *(see Lk 22.37).*

end of a stick. Then he held it up to Jesus' lips and said, "Wait! Let us see if Elijah is coming to bring him down from the cross!"

[37] With a loud cry Jesus died.

[38] The curtain hanging in the Temple was torn in two, from top to bottom. [39] The army officer who was standing there in front of the cross saw how Jesus had died. [a] "This man was really the Son of God!" he said.

[40] Some women were there, looking on from a distance. Among them were Mary Magdalene, Mary the mother of the younger James and of Joseph, and Salome. [41] They had followed Jesus while he was in Galilee and had helped him. Many other women who had come to Jerusalem with him were there also.

The Burial of Jesus

[42-43] It was towards evening when Joseph of Arimathea arrived. He was a respected member of the Council, who was waiting for the coming of the Kingdom of God. It was Preparation day (that is, the day before the Sabbath), so Joseph went boldly into the presence of Pilate and asked him for the body of Jesus. [44] Pilate was surprised to hear that Jesus was already dead. He called the army officer and asked him if Jesus had been dead a long time.

a 15.39 had died; *some manuscripts have* had cried out and died.

[45] After hearing the officer's report, Pilate told Joseph he could have the body. [46] Joseph bought a linen sheet, took the body down, wrapped it in the sheet, and placed it in a tomb which had been dug out of solid rock. Then he rolled a large stone across the entrance to the tomb. [47] Mary Magdalene and Mary the mother of Joseph were watching and saw where the body of Jesus was placed.

The Resurrection

16 After the Sabbath was over, Mary Magdalene, Mary the mother of James, and Salome bought spices to go and anoint the body of Jesus. [2] Very early on Sunday morning, at sunrise, they went to the tomb. [3-4] On the way they said to one another, "Who will roll away the stone for us from the entrance to the tomb?" (It was a very large stone.) Then they looked up and saw that the stone had already been rolled back. [5] So they entered the tomb, where they saw a young man sitting on the right, wearing a white robe – and they were alarmed.

[6] "Don't be alarmed," he said. "I know you are looking for Jesus of Nazareth, who was crucified. He is not here – he has been raised! Look, here is the place where they put him. [7] Now go and give this message to his disciples, including Peter: 'He is going to Galilee ahead of you; there you will see him, just as he told you.' "

⁸ So they went out and ran from the tomb, distressed and terrified. They said nothing to anyone, because they were afraid.

An Old Ending to the Gospel ª
16.9–20

Jesus Appears to Mary Magdalene

[⁹ After Jesus rose from death early on Sunday, he appeared first to Mary Magdalene, from whom he had driven out seven demons. ¹⁰ She went and told his companions. They were mourning and crying; ¹¹ and when they heard her say that Jesus was alive and that she had seen him, they did not believe her.

Jesus Appears to Two Disciples

¹² After this, Jesus appeared in a different manner to two of them while they were on their way to the country. ¹³ They returned and told the others, but they would not believe it.

Jesus Appears to the Eleven

¹⁴ Last of all, Jesus appeared to the eleven disciples as

a 16.9–20 heading *Some manuscripts and ancient translations do not have this ending to the Gospel (verses 9–20).*

they were eating. He scolded them, because they did not have faith and because they were too stubborn to believe those who had seen him alive. [15] He said to them, "Go throughout the whole world and preach the gospel to the whole human race. [16] Whoever believes and is baptized will be saved; whoever does not believe will be condemned. [17] Believers will be given the power to perform miracles: they will drive out demons in my name; they will speak in strange tongues; [18] if they pick up snakes or drink any poison, they will not be harmed; they will place their hands on sick people, who will get well."

Jesus is Taken Up to Heaven

[19] After the Lord Jesus had talked with them, he was taken up to heaven and sat at the right side of God. [20] The disciples went and preached everywhere, and the Lord worked with them and proved that their preaching was true by the miracles that were performed.]

Another Old Ending [a]

16.9–10

[⁹ The women went to Peter and his friends and gave them a brief account of all they had been told. ¹⁰ After this, Jesus himself sent out through his disciples from the east to the west the sacred and ever-living message of eternal salvation.]

a 16.9–10 heading *Some manuscripts and ancient translations have this shorter ending to the Gospel in addition to the longer ending (verses 9–20).*

Also available in the same series:

LIFELINES

edited by Chris Gidney

The Story of Wendy Craig

I recognized that it was a strange emptiness within that had finally boiled up like a huge tumour inside me. I would constantly try and analyse this feeling until I sat down in the garden one day and asked God if he could please tell me what was going on.

Wendy Craig, TV mum from the classic series *Not in Front of the Children*, *And Mother Makes Three* and *Butterflies*, grew up believing in Jesus. But a busy family life and her acting career soon squeezed out her faith.

Many years later she came to a point of crisis and realized she had lost something important in her life, and desperately needed to find it again.

In this *Lifelines* book, meet Wendy Craig, TV actress and writer, who recovered a faith lost from childhood. Wendy's story is followed by the story which inspires her life – the Gospel of Mark.

Also by Chris Gidney and available from HarperCollins:

Street Life
The Bryan Mosley Story
by Chris Gidney

When Bryan Mosley set out to be an actor, he little knew that he would become one of the most instantly recognized characters on television. As a young man he had a passion for acting and applied to drama school. But within a few years he was married with six children to support and the unknown, but talented, actor was desperate to find the right openings in theatre, TV, or film work. In 1961, Bryan's big break came when he auditioned for the role of Alf Roberts in the fledgling TV series, *Coronation Street*.

For thirty-eight years Alf was a regular part of Britain's most popular soap. His face was familiar to 20 million viewers each week. But the real-life Bryan was very different from the grumpy, flustered buffoon he played. *Street Life* tells of a man with a deep sense of humour, sensitivity and compassion for others. Bryan was remarkable in show business for his lifelong devotion to his wife and family and for his unshakeable Christian faith.

Publishing in April 2000:

Rock on, Tommy!

Tommy Cannon and Bobby Ball
with Chris Gidney

Tommy Cannon and Bobby Ball broke all records for capacity audiences at the London Palladium and starred in the longest running show in Blackpool. They are still doing summer seasons and pantomime seasons each year as well as their gospel shows. In this book they tell their own story.

Tommy and Bobby met in 1964 when they were both very young and working in a factory. It was to be the start of a lifelong friendship and a double act that would soon turn professional. The famous duo chart their careers; the laughter and pain along the way; the changes that conversion to Christian faith brought for both of them. And it is all told in their honest, blunt, down-to-earth style.

Little Goes a Long Way
My Own Story
Syd Little

Few comedy duos have brought more pleasure to more people than Little and Large. From their long-running television series to their frequent live performances, millions have grown up with their unique brand of humour.

Syd Little has risen from very ordinary roots to the pinnacle of show business, and has worked with the very best entertainers. But success and laughter have only been half of it. Syd has had more than his fair share of tragedy and tears. His son's tragic battle with drugs and other personal struggles have been as tough to bear as they are dramatic. Now he tells for the first time the secret of how he made it through.